# Mauzy's
## Depression Era
# Kitchen Glass

### Barbara and
### Jim Mauzy

Schiffer
Publishing Ltd

4880 Lower Valley Road, Atglen, PA 19310 USA

Layout by "Sue"
Type set in Tango BT/Korinna BT

ISBN: 0-7643-2555-8
Printed in China

Published by Schiffer Publishing Ltd.
4880 Lower Valley Road
Atglen, PA 19310
Phone: (610) 593-1777; Fax: (610) 593-2002
E-mail: Info@schifferbooks.com

For the largest selection of fine reference books on this and
related subjects, please visit our web site at
**www.schifferbooks.com**
We are always looking for people to write books on new and
related subjects. If you have an idea for a book please
contact us at the above address.

This book may be purchased from the publisher.
Include $3.95 for shipping.
Please try your bookstore first.
You may write for a free catalog.

In Europe, Schiffer books are distributed by
Bushwood Books
6 Marksbury Ave.
Kew Gardens
Surrey TW9 4JF England
Phone: 44 (0) 20 8392-8585; Fax: 44 (0) 20 8392-9876
E-mail: info@bushwoodbooks.co.uk
Website: www.bushwoodbooks.co.uk
Free postage in the U.K., Europe; air mail at cost.

# Contents

# Dedication

For Michael Adam Mauzy...our first grandson who entered this world while we were working on the pages of this book. Michael brings more sparkle into our lives than any piece of glass within these pages. Welcome, little man! Grandma and Grandpa love you.

# Acknowledgments

The pages of this book are exploding with fabulous, interesting, and colorful examples of vintage kitchen glass because of the generosity of the people listed below. They have donated more than just their wonderful glassware; they have shared information, insight, and an enthusiasm that we have attempted to bring to each page. We humbly acknowledge that without these awesome people, and a few who have remained anonymous, *Mauzy's Depression Era Kitchen Glass* would be blank pages. We thank all of you for allowing all of us to enjoy your treasures.

Todd Baum and Jesse Speicher
Joycelyn and Parke Bloyer
Francee Boches, Cheshire Cat Antiques
Dennis A. Busold, Robin's Nest Antiques
Joyce and Jim Coverston, The Attic Annex
Clark Crawford
Ron and Sue Dibeler
Russ and Ann Dippon
Kathy and Tom Donlan
David and Maryann Gaydos
Gary Geiselman
Keith and Judy Hendrix
Kane's Antiques
Cheryl Kevish
Charles and Susan Keye
Carol Korn
Gary and Donna Kovar
Walt Lemiski – Waltz Time Antiques.
Arnie Messoner
Sharon M. McGuire

Fred McMorrow and Rodger Daye
Dr. Dominic J. Menta
David Mitchell
Jack and Joyce Nichols
Sharon Nueske
Linda and Ron Peterson
Bill Phillips
Cheryl and "Tab" Powell
Dave and Hilda Proctor
Edity Putanko (owner of) Edie's Glassware
Barbara Quick and Milton Quick
Dave Renner
Julia & Jim Retzloff
Glen and Carolyn Robinson
Faye and Robert Smith
Lynn and Faye Strait
Jan Wright
John and Marilyn Yallop
Terry and Don Yusko
Aniceta Zamborsky

Our thanks also are extended to the Depression Glass Clubs and show promoters who have had us as guests and given us the opportunity to photograph at their events. We depend on this networking with collectors and dealers alike to report values that are as accurate as possible, and to meet with serious collectors who are indeed the real experts.

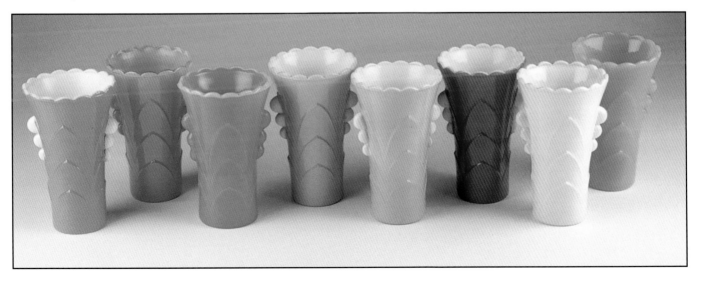

# Preface

Dear Readers,

    As collectors and dealers we look upon the subject of kitchen glass as one of our favorites and hope that this shows on each and every page. We offered our first book on this subject in 2004 knowing it was incomplete, but regarding it as both a valiant effort and a way to communicate to dealers and collectors alike how extremely interested in and knowledgeable of kitchen glass we were. That book was a start, and this book is a continuation. We are happy to present this second volume with virtually **no repetition** from the first book. This volume offers all new examples, all new pictures, all new information. If you love kitchen glass the way we do, you will want, no, you will need both books, as each stands totally alone in merit and material.

    Now that the Glass World knows how serious we are about kitchen glass, we look forward to additional books with even more glassware. If you have pieces that we haven't presented, and we know there are thousands of you who do, and you can bring your glassware to the studio in south central Pennsylvania, let us know! You can also talk to your Depression Glass Show Committee and show promoters about having us as guests at an event. We hope to have your name listed in the next book we publish.

    Meanwhile, put the elegant glass back in the cabinet, walk away from the formality of the dining room, grab a mug of coffee or tea, and flop down at your kitchen table and rediscover why the kitchen always has been the heart of the home, and fall in love with kitchen glass all over again.

Barbara and Jim
Mauzy
**www.TPTT.net**

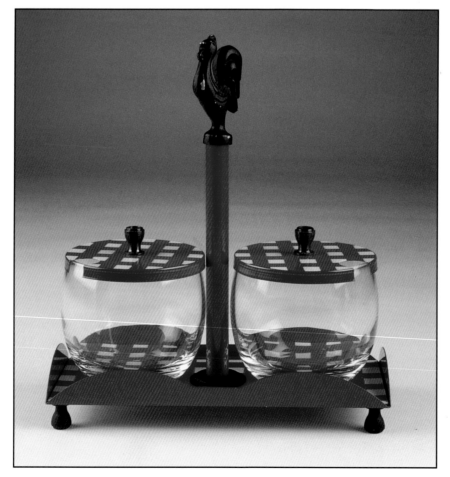

# About the Glass

Free! Yes, free! So much of the collectible glassware from the Depression Era was free or oh-so-inexpensive. After the crash of the New York Stock Market in 1929 America's economy spiraled into a depression that took years and lots of government programming to resolve.

Depression Era glassware, both tableware (see *Mauzy's Depression Glass*) and kitchen glass, were mass-produced with virtually no concern with quality. After all, so much of this glassware would be given to a consumer free or inexpensively with the purchase of a good or service: buy cereal and get a creamer or sugar bowl for free, buy flour and get a mixing bowl for free. What remains is a legacy of American design in a huge palette of transparent and opaque colors that was created simply to entice the homemaker to reach into her wallet and spend money during a period of time when there was little or, possibly, next to nothing in that wallet.

Today there are two groups of thought regarding the colorful glassware from decades past. One group is amazed that the junky glass Grandma had is worth anything at all, let alone some of the values listed here. The other group embraces the usefulness and beauty of the bowls, reamers, containers, and more, not merely as kitchen decorations but as tools to be utilized in the twenty-first century.

One cannot ever lose sight of the history that characterizes this glass. It was free or inexpensive, and poor quality control resulted in glassware with all sorts of irregularities as made: lines that look like cracks, but aren't, inconsistencies in coloration, bumps and dents in the glass itself, dirt molded inside the glass, and so on. Add to this the simple fact that kitchen glassware was used. Grandma may have had eight dinner plates, but she probably only used those on the top of the stack, therefore never- or barely-used plates might have remained at the bottom for us to appreciate today. Such is not the case with kitchen glass. The pieces shown within these pages were essential to prepare a meal and store the leftovers and used they were.

As indispensable tools kitchen glassware was utilized each time a meal was prepared. From a collectible standpoint one must determine one's own definitions of use and abuse, as there is a difference. It is virtually impossible to find a refrigerator dish without some nicking along the rim and lid. There is a vast difference between some roughness that catches a fingernail and a chip that might slice one's skin. However, embrace the flaws that are intrinsic to vintage kitchen glassware. After all, if you want perfect, go to the mall; if you want the real deal you simply have to have realistic expectations.

It is not uncommon to find foreign matter imbedded in vintage kitchen glass. As mass produced glassware that often given away quality control was minimal at best.

Nothing made Mother happier than wonderful kitchenware! Just ask the manufacturers who advertised most heavily in women's magazines in May and June during wedding season, and in December for Christmas gift giving. The delighted faces on the Mixmaster brochure say it all!

This book showcases glassware from almost one hundred different manufacturers. All competed for a piece of the marketplace and whenever one company offered something that was successful many others du-

# Keep your **MIXMASTER** out

Mixmaster occupies a small amount of space in your kitchen, therefore, you should keep it readily accessible. Keep it where it is convenient to use at a moment's notice at all times. In this way you will use it for every meal, every day and save yourself more time and arm-work. One of the first things you should do is select or prepare a good, permanent location for your Mixmaster, a place where it will always be plugged in ready for instant use at the turn of the switch. A double outlet for this purpose is inexpensive and convenient.

*Made and Guaranteed by*

**CHICAGO FLEXIBLE SHAFT COMPANY**
**5600 W. ROOSEVELT ROAD**
CHICAGO, ILLINOIS

*Over Half a Century Making Quality Products*

5503G

plicated the glass as closely as patent law allowed. Today we are left with a vast array of wonderful treasures from kitchens past. The coffee carafe shown in the Glasbake brochure is featured on page 134 in white and, today, remains as useful as it is collectible. Sunbeam is still producing new mixers, plus they are refurbishing and selling old Mixmasters. That's how dependable they are. If we interpreted the coding on the cover of Sunbeam's document, it is from 1955 and the model shown is featured on page 86.

Cook with **GLASBAKE** and **RANGE-TEC**

*A little care means years of wear from your McKee Glassware*

Make your work in the kitchen easier, —insure tastier, more delicious dishes by using Glasbake and Range-tec glass utensils. Easy to clean, these bright attractive utensils permit you to "look while you cook" and to serve at the table from the same dish in which you cook.

**McKEE GLASS COMPANY**
JEANNETTE, PA.          ESTABLISHED 1853

**Additional items of Glasbake Ovenware and Range-tec Top of Stove Ware may be purchased from your local chain and department stores.**

Copyright 1946 McKee Glass Co.          Lithographed in U.S.A.

# About the Book and the Prices

This book will beautifully accompany our first book on kitchen glass, *Mauzy's Kitchen Glass,* with virtually no pieces of kitchen glass from the 1920s-1950s duplicated in this second volume. Even with two books the presentation is still not fully inclusive, but these pages offer a showcase of vintage glass that is lovely to see, easy to use, and interesting to collect as we continue to explore this area. We are planning additional volumes and in fact have already begun the photographic efforts.

We have done everything possible to provide accurate prices by monitoring the Internet, auctions, and trade papers, going to shows, and consulting with collectors and dealers alike. To this effort we bring years of buying, selling, and collecting kitchen glassware, a personal favorite of ours. Values vary immensely according to the condition of the piece, the location of the market, and the overall quality of the design and manufacture. Condition is always of paramount importance when assigning a value. The prices shown in this reference are for individual items that are in mint condition, but not packaged. When glassware retains original stickers or the original box the value is enhanced. Prices in the Midwest differ from those in the West or East, and those at specialty shows such as Depression Glass shows will vary from those at general shows. And, of course, being at the right place at the right time can make all the difference.

All of these factors make it impossible to create an absolutely accurate price list, but we can offer a guide. The values shown in this reference reflect what one could realistically expect to pay but ultimately the seller and the buyer determine values as they agree upon a price.

*Neither the authors nor the publisher are responsible for any outcomes resulting from this reference.*

# Kitchen Glass by Color

Pitcher and tumbler. Westmoreland Glass Company. Referred to as "Scramble" but not the actual name, this 1802/1821/ ½ Gallon Covered Ice Tea pitcher and tumbler were sold as a set consisting of the covered pitcher and six tumblers. The value of the pitcher is largely in its cover. Pitcher with lid, $85; pitcher without lid, $35; tumblers, $8 each.

Cruet. Unknown manufacturer. One of the earliest pieces in this book, the 6.5" tall cruet dates to about 1910. $50. *Courtesy of Walt Lemiski – Waltz Time Antiques.*

Jar, shaker, and mug. Unknown manufacturers. What looks like a canister is actually a Tobacco Jar. The 5.25" tall shaker features an interesting horseshoe motif. The beer mug is 3.5" deep and 2.75" in diameter. Jar, $60; shaker, $50; mug, $25. *Courtesy of Walt Lemiski – Waltz Time Antiques.*

Shakers, canisters, and salt box. Sneath Glass Company of Hartford City, Indiana. This Amber Napanee set consists of the following: round stippled cracker jar, 7.25" high; 7" COFFEE jar, 5.25" TEA jar, 4.25" spice jars and shakers, and a 6.5" long x 3.5" wide x 3" deep SALT box that never had a lid. The cracker jar is shown with a tin lid. Check the Peacock Blue glass for a cracker jar with the decorative lid. A complete set as shown is quite rare, and seeing these pieces together reveals the variation in color even within a single manufacturer. Cracker jar, $500; stand, $40; coffee and tea canisters, $275 each; spice jars and shakers, $75 each; salt box, $200.

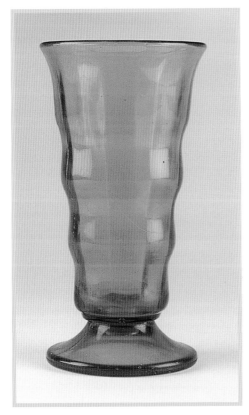

Cheese dish. Unknown manufacturer. Made in England, the 4.5" tall lid rests on a 9.5" x 6" base. $50. *Courtesy of Walt Lemiski – Waltz Time Antiques.*

Stirrers. Various manufacturers. Little information exists regarding the manufacturing of glass swizzle sticks and stirrers. The original patent for swizzle sticks was for a wooden spear-like stick for stabbing a cherry or olive in a martini. Left, $20; others, $5 each. *Courtesy of Walt Lemiski – Waltz Time Antiques.*

Sundae glass. Paden City. Measuring 7" tall with a 3.75" diameter, this ice cream sundae glass is in demand in any color. $25. *Courtesy of Walt Lemiski – Waltz Time Antiques.*

Bottle. McKee Glass
Company. 9.5" tall. $35.
*Courtesy of Walt Lemiski –
Waltz Time Antiques.*

Ladles. The Cambridge Glass Company. Both spoons are about 5" long. $20
each. *Courtesy of Walt Lemiski – Waltz Time Antiques.*

Whip. Federal
Glass Company.
The whip was
used to make
mayonnaise and is
3" deep and 4.5"
in diameter. The
top is marked,
"CHICAGO
PRECISION
PRODUCTS
CORP. CHICAGO,
ILL. PAT. APLD."
$60. *Courtesy of
Walt Lemiski –
Waltz Time
Antiques.*

Measuring cup
and reamer.
Federal Glass
Company. The
one-cup measure
was sold as "2539
Handled Measur-
ing Cup." The
reamer was part
of a fifteen-piece
kitchen set.
Federal used the
term "Golden
Glow" rather than
"amber" to
describe this
color. Measuring
cup, $65; reamer,
$55. *Courtesy of
Clark Crawford.*

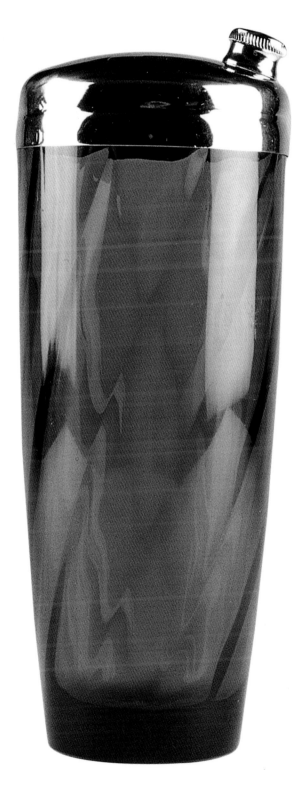

Shakers. Unknown manufacture. Just over 2" in height, these appear to be ruby, but when placed in a strong light they are a true amethyst color. The lids are plastic. $75.

Cocktail Shaker. Continental Can. The HAZEL Ware line includes many pieces of Moroccan Amethyst dinnerware (See *Mauzy's Depression Glass*) including the 9" tall cocktail shaker. $70. *Courtesy of Walt Lemiski – Waltz Time Antiques.*

Mayonnaise comport. L.E. Smith Glass Company. The comport and under plate are part of the "Melba" dinnerware line. Most of the pieces are octagonal, but some are round and ruffled. Comport, $35; under plate, $10; spoon, $8. *Courtesy of Walt Lemiski – Waltz Time Antiques.*

# Black

Ashtrays. Imperial Glass. The box of four ashtrays is marked "Imperial Glass by Lenox" and the back of each piece has the Imperial marking. Designed for use at a bridge party or poker game the 3" x 3.5" ashtrays are whimsically named "The Winning Hand." $10 each. Add $20 for a box in perfect condition.

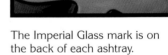

The Imperial Glass mark is on the back of each ashtray.

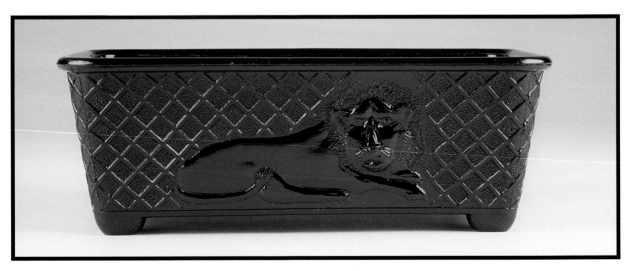

Window box planter. McKee Glass Company. This is 5" x 9" x 3" deep. $125. *Courtesy of Todd Baum and Jesse Speicher.*

Vases and candy jar. McKee Glass Company. When a lid is placed on the 7.5" tall No. 100 "Triangle" vase it becomes a candy jar. Variations in height and nude versus dressed add to the values of Triangle vases. Left to right: nude 8.5" tall vase, $275; 7.5" base, $200; lid, $225, dressed 8.5" vase; $275. *Courtesy of Todd Baum and Jesse Speicher.*

Sundae glass. Unknown manufacturer. Marked "VEECUP CHICAGO 316P" this 5.5" tall, 3.25" diameter glass was designed to hold a cone-shaped paper cup into which an ice cream sundae would be made. $35. *Courtesy of Walt Lemiski – Waltz Time Antiques.*

Lid. McKee Glass Company. This stacked lid transforms a 7.5" "Triangle" vase into a candy jar. $225. *Courtesy of Todd Baum and Jesse Speicher.*

Cocktail tumbler. McKee Glass Company. The 3.25" tall "bottoms up" cocktail tumbler is shown with split legs, and originally sold for $1.00 each. $225. *Courtesy of Todd Baum and Jesse Speicher.*

Planters and vase. McKee Glass Company. Back: 8" tall Sarah vase. Front row from early 1930s, left: 5.25" deep, 6" diameter No. 25 Three-Footed Jardinière. If this had a lid it would become the No. 25 Three-Footed Cookie Jar and Cover. Front row, middle: 2.25" deep, 5.5" diameter No. 27 bulb bowl; right: 3.25" deep, 7" diameter No. 26 bulb bowl. Vase: $175; bulb bowlsand jardinere $75 each; lid, $100; cookie jar, $175. *Courtesy of Todd Baum and Jesse Speicher.*

Cookie jars. The L.E. Smith Glass Company. Both jars are 6.75" in diameter, but one is 3.5" deep and the other is 8.25" deep. The taller jar on the right was the No. 3 Cookie Jar advertised to have a nine-pound capacity and available with hand-painted flowers on one side. $75 each. *Courtesy of Walt Lemiski – Waltz Time Antiques.*

Shakers. McKee Glass Company. The four shakers shown were introduced in white as the "4 Piece Kitchen Shaker Set" at a price of $1.40 per set in 1931. McKee Glass Company began offering black glassware in 1930, so one can assume these shakers were probably also available in 1931 along with the black McKee vases introduced that same year. The value of these shakers is dependent on the quality of the lettering and original metal tops, not just on the condition of the glass. Pepper, $50; Salt, $70; Flour and Sugar, $85 each. *Courtesy of Tom Donlan.*

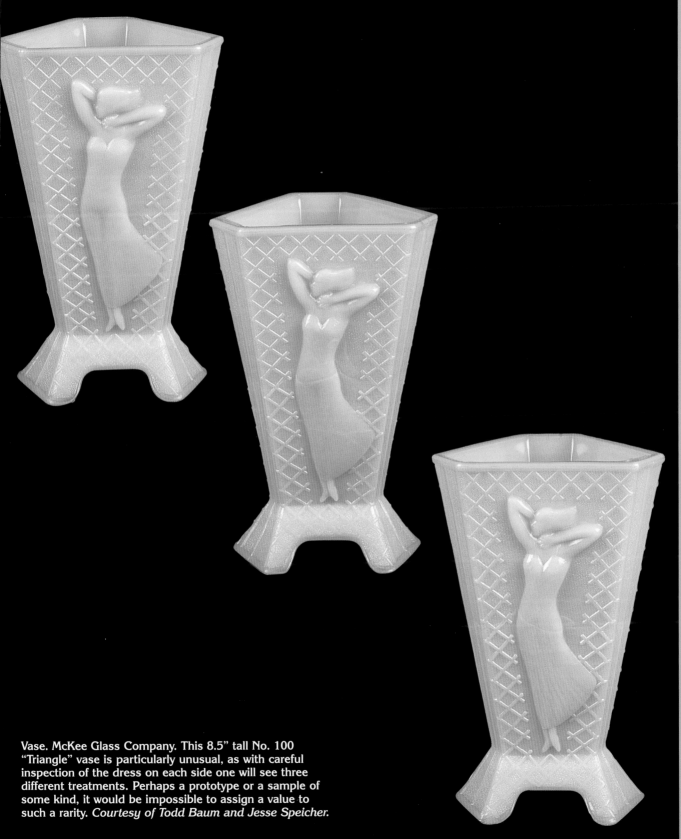

# Blue – Chalaine

Vase. McKee Glass Company. This 8.5" tall No. 100 "Triangle" vase is particularly unusual, as with careful inspection of the dress on each side one will see three different treatments. Perhaps a prototype or a sample of some kind, it would be impossible to assign a value to such a rarity. *Courtesy of Todd Baum and Jesse Speicher.*

Vases and bulb bowl. McKee Glass Company. 8.5" "Triangle" vases are shown with nude and dressed figures. The 5.5" diameter, 2.5" deep bulb bowl is item No. 26. Nude vase, $600; dressed vase, $750; bulb bowl, $85. *Courtesy of Todd Baum and Jesse Speicher.*

Vase. McKee Glass Company. The "Modern Square" design is on this 7.75" tall, 7.75" diameter vase. $450. *Courtesy of Todd Baum and Jesse Speicher.*

Vase. McKee Glass Company. 8" tall Sarah vase. $175. *Courtesy of Todd Baum and Jesse Speicher.*

Bowl. Manning-Bowman. This is the larger of two bowls designed for use with an electric mixer measuring 9" in diameter and 4.5" deep. $150. *Courtesy of Walt Lemiski – Waltz Time Antiques.*

The manufacturer's information is on the bottom of the bowl.

Bowl. Manning-Bowman. This is the smaller of two bowls designed for use with an electric mixer measuring 6.5" in diameter and 4.5" deep. $150. *Courtesy of Todd Baum and Jesse Speicher.*

# Blue - Cobalt

Vase. McKee Glass Company. This is thought to be the only "Triangle" vase made in cobalt blue. Supposedly a worker in the factory made this and stealthily carried it home in his lunch pail, making it most definitely too rare to price. *Courtesy of Todd Baum and Jesse Speicher.*

Pitcher and tumblers. Hazel-Atlas. Originally issued in green in 1930, the 1488 Pressed Ice Lip Pitcher features a diamond optic. The tumblers are 5.25" tall with a 3" diameter and 4" tall with a 2.75" diameter. Pitcher, $50; tumbler, $10. *Courtesy of David and Maryann Gaydos.*

Pitcher and tumblers. Hazel-Atlas. The 9937 "Fine Ribbed" tilt pitcher holds 80 ounces and is about 6.5" tall to the spout. There are three sizes – iced tea (shown), water, and juice – but there have been reports of a possible fourth size. Any information on these pitchers would be welcome. The tumblers are shown in the three sizes we know of: 3.25" tall, 2.25" diameter; 4" tall, 2.75" diameter; and 5" tall, 3" diameter. The pitchers and tumblers were also made in pink and crystal (clear) and are from the mid- to late-1930s. $50. *Courtesy of David and Maryann Gaydos.*

Decanter and tumbler. Unknown manufacturer. This design has come to be called "Ring of Rings" and features a 10" tall decanter and 3" tall whiskey tumblers. Decanter, $85; tumbler, $10. *Courtesy of Walt Lemiski – Waltz Time Antiques.*

Water bottle. Hazel-Atlas Glass Company. 9.5" tall, this bottle is marked with the following: "DESIGN PATENT 93752." $85. *Courtesy of Walt Lemiski – Waltz Time Antiques.*

# Blue - Delphite

Baking dish, pie plate, and bowl. PYREX® by Corning Glass Works. All of this light blue Delphite is marked "Made in U.S.A." The baking dish is 10" in diameter handle to handle and 3" deep, and comes with a clear lid. The pie plate is almost 10.5" in diameter, and the 9" square "Hostess" bowl is 3.25" deep. The Hostess bowl is commonly-found in opal with red or yellow; Delphite is quite rare. $175 each. *Courtesy of Todd Baum and Jesse Speicher.*

Bowls. PYREX® by Corning Glass Works. All of this dark blue Delphite is marked "Made in Canada." The largest bowl is 11.5" in diameter and 4.25" deep with a square base. The 10" diameter, 3.75" deep bowl and 7" diameter, 3" deep bowl each have a round base. $175 each. *Courtesy of Todd Baum / Jesse Speicher.*

Vase, plate, refrigerator dish, and bowl. Anchor Hocking Glass Company, McKee Glass Company, and unknown manufacturer. The 5.25" tall vase is a Fire-King "Deco" vase that was made in many other colors. The 9.5" plate is a piece of Canadian restaurantware by an unknown manufacturer. The 5" x 4.25" x 2.5" deep refrigerator dish is a McKee item as is the 7.5" diameter, 3.25" deep bowl. Vase, $75; plate, $175; refrigerator dish, $70; bowl, $175. *Courtesy of Todd Baum / Jesse Speicher.*

Pitcher. PYREX® by Macbeth-Evans Division of Corning Glass Works. Made in Canada, the "Piecrust" 5.25" tall pitcher is part of a dinnerware line of the same name. $45. *Courtesy of Walt Lemiski – Waltz Time Antiques.*

# Blue — Ice

Knife. Probably Dur-X. 9.25" in length, this is marked "MADE IN U.S.A." on one side and "PAT. PEND." on the other. $45. *Courtesy of Walt Lemiski – Waltz Time Antiques.*

# Blue — Miscellaneous

Ladle. Unknown manufacturer. 5" long. $45. *Courtesy of Walt Lemiski – Waltz Time Antiques.*

Jars. Unknown manufacturer. The 6" tall jar has a "C" on the bottom, and the 4.5" tall jar has "10" on the bottom. $10 each. *Courtesy of Walt Lemiski – Waltz Time Antiques.*

# Blue — Peacock

Vase. McKee Glass Company. The dressed figure on any 8.5" tall "Triangle" vase is more difficult to find than a nude, but nothing is easily found in this color. $1000. *Courtesy of Todd Baum and Jesse Speicher.*

Cruet. Fenton Art Glass. Opalescent hobnail is a trademark of Fenton. This cruet is 4.5" tall to the top of the stopper. $30. *Courtesy of Walt Lemiski – Waltz Time Antiques.X*

Syrup pitcher and drip plate. Paden City Glass Manufacturing Company. The pitcher measures 4.25" tall at the handle and rests on a 5.5" under plate with a 2.75" center indent. The lid greatly enhances the value of this three-piece set. $185. *Courtesy of David and Maryann Gaydos.*

Jam jar. Unknown manufacturer. This is 4" tall and 3.5" diameter with a matching ladle. Jar, $65; ladle, $35. *Courtesy of David and Maryann Gaydos.*

Canisters and salt box. Sneath Glass Company of Hartford City, Indiana. This Colonial Pattern set consists of the following: round cracker jar, 7.25" high; 7" coffee jar, 5" tea jar, 4.5" spice jars, and a 3.5" wide, 2" deep salt box that never had a lid and is the smallest of the "Hoosier" salts. The cracker jar is shown with a decorative lid. Check the Amber glass for a Sneath cracker jar with the tin lid. A complete set as shown is quite rare. The glass rings encircling each item allows the glassware to be suspended in a holder without falling through. Cracker jar, $700; stand, $40; coffee and tea canisters, $475 each; spice jars and shakers, $125 each; salt box, $350.

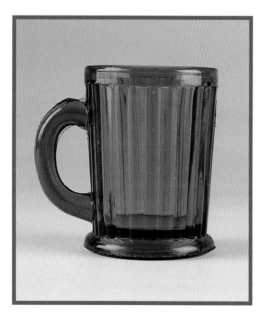

Mug. Unknown manufacturer. Small in size, this is only 3" tall and 2.25" in diameter, $20. *Courtesy of Walt Lemiski – Waltz Time Antiques.*

Provisions jars. Unknown manufacturer. Both canisters have ground rims and lids. They are 5.5" tall with a 4.25" diameter and 4" tall with a 3.5" diameter. $70 each. *Courtesy of Walt Lemiski – Waltz Time Antiques.*

Jardinière, cocktail tumbler, coaster. McKee Glass Company. The 6" diameter, 5.5" deep three-footed No. 25 jardinière is rarely seen in this color that McKee called "Old Rose." The 3.25" tall "bottoms up" cocktail tumbler is shown with the legs together next to its 4" diameter coaster. Jardinière, $95; tumbler, $175; coaster, $175. *Courtesy of Todd Baum and Jesse Speicher.*

Reamers. Jeannette Glass Company. Made of slag glass in dark caramel, these are Fleur-de-lis reamers. They are quite fragile due to the manufacturing process in which they are heated and reheated. Few are found in good condition, and no two are ever the same. $650 each. *Courtesy of Arnie Messoner.*

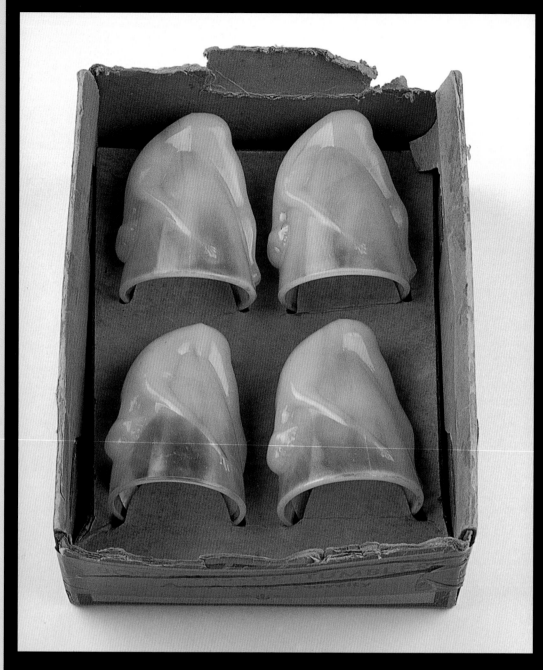

Bottoms-up tumblers. McKee Glass Company. Although ragged and repaired, an original box for these cocktail shakers is rarely found. The side panels read: "IDEAL PRIZE FOR [can't read this word] CARD PARTIES, CARNIVALS, PICNICS, ETC. THE TUMBLER WITH A BOTTOM BUT *TRY* TO MAKE IT STAND. BOTTOMS UP TUMBLER An Artistic Novelty." These tumblers were introduced in 1932, and they sold for $1.00 each. The opalescence of these tumblers is particularly unusual. $125 each. Add $35 for box in "as is" condition. *Courtesy of Faye and Robert Smith.*

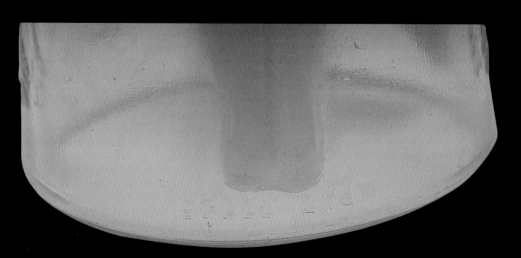

**The patent date below the feet distinguishes old bottoms up tumblers from reproductions.**

Lids. Cupples Company, St. Louis. 2.5" diameter top seals for canning are marked "Presto TO OPEN INSERT KNIFE AT NOTCH PAT RE 17562." Twelve No. 10 glass lids cost $.29. The value of this item is because of the package has survived unscathed. $20 as shown. Individual lids would be worth about $1.

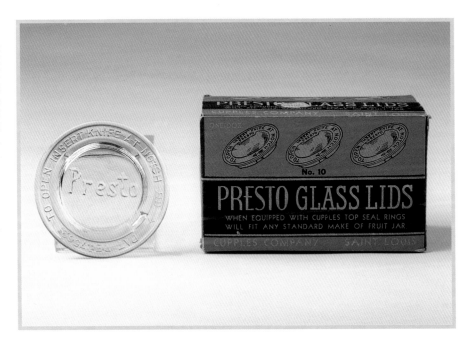

Measuring cup. Unknown manufacturer. There is no manufacturing information on this one-cup measure that includes increments for cups in quarters, thirds, and ounces. "WESSON OIL" is embossed on the bottom leading one to presume this was free or very inexpensive with the purchase of Wesson Oil. Clear measuring cups are usually of little value, but the advertising connection enhances the value of this 3.5" tall measure. $35.

Measuring cup. McKee Glass Company. Glasbake was a McKee line of ovenware. Complete with an unusual spout design, this four-cup measure is 4" tall at the handle. Increments for cups and ounces are on both sides. The base is marked: "J-2031 12." $30.
*Courtesy of Joycelyn and Parke Bloyer*

Close up of bottom mark.

Measuring cup. Unknown manufacturer. Made for Sellers kitchen cabinets, a one-cup measure is 2.75" tall and 3" in diameter. The bottom is marked "SELLERS PAT. – APLD FOR." *Courtesy of Aniceta Zamborsky.*

Measuring cup and pitcher. Hazel-Atlas Glass Company and unknown manufacturer. The two-cup measure is 3.75" deep and 4.5" in diameter. The base is marked, "SPRY MEASURING MIXING PITCHER." The 5.5" tall pitcher has a diameter of 4.75". It is a Hazel-Atlas item that is also marked "A&J" indicating an A&J beater was designed to fit on top, $20 each. *Courtesy of Walt Lemiski – Waltz Time Antiques.*

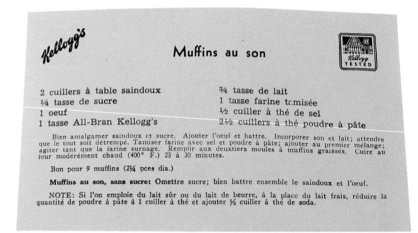

Each measuring cup included a recipe card. One side is in English, the other in French for distribution in Quebec, Canada. *Courtesy of Walt Lemiski – Waltz Time Antiques.*

Measuring cup. Unknown manufacturer. A 3.5" tall one-cup measure was free with the purchase of Kellogg's All-Bran cereal. $20 each. Add $40 for the original box. *Courtesy of Walt Lemiski – Waltz Time Antiques.*

Measures. Unknown manufacturers. Ounces are measured in the "Juices" glass while tablespoons are measured in the "Sugar" glass. One can assume these were for use in mixing cocktails. $15 each. *Courtesy of Walt Lemiski – Waltz Time Antiques.*

Measuring cups. Unknown manufacturers. Left to right: "IMPERIAL MEASURE" with increments for half-pints and every ten ounces. This handled container is 5.5" deep and 5.25" in diameter with the following markings on the base: "T&S TORRINGTON HANDIMAID FOR DOMESTIC USE ONLY MADE IN U.S.A." The lip along the top rim is for securing a beater top. The measuring cup in the middle has a textured surface and is 5.5" deep and 4.5" in diameter. Pints, cups, and every four ounces are shown on one side. The measure without a handle is 4.5" deep and 4.5" in diameter with quarter-pints, half-cups, and every four ounces shown on one side. $20 each. *Courtesy of Walt Lemiski – Waltz Time Antiques.*

Pitcher and tumblers. Hocking Glass Company. This is one of the vast combinations of colorful striped glassware made by Hocking in the 1930s. Pitcher, $35; tumblers, $8 each. *Courtesy of Walt Lemiski – Waltz Time Antiques.*

Pitchers. Hazel-Atlas Glass Company and Hocking Glass Company. The 80-ounce "Blown Water Pitcher" on the left is the larger 8.25" tall size; a matching juice pitcher with a capacity of 40 ounces was also produced by Hazel-Atlas. These were manufactured in the 1930s. The Hocking pitcher is 8" tall. Hazel-Atlas, $50; Hocking, $25. *Courtesy of Walt Lemiski – Waltz Time Antiques.*

Pitcher. Federal Glass Company. The 7" tall, 60-ounce pitcher was free with the purchase of "9 Complexion Size Bars of New Creamy Fragrance Camay at Regular Price" of sixty-six cents. This is part of the "Star" pattern made by Federal in the 1950s. $15; $45 as shown.

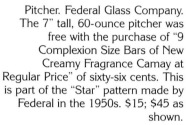

Mold. Sanitary Food Molds. 5.5" diameter, 3" deep. The bottom is marked: "TRADE MARK REG. KOLD OR HOT UTILITY GLASS APP FOR US PAT OFF." $15. Note that this has a light green hue that becomes yellowish in sunlight.

Mold. Unknown manufacturer. From England, a 5.25" x 3.25" jelly or jell-o mold has an intricate design along the rim. $25. *Courtesy of Walt Lemiski – Waltz Time Antiques.*

Vase & tumbler. McKee Glass Company. Because the 7.5" tall "Triangle" vase and 3.25" tall "bottoms up" cocktail tumbler are difficult to find in crystal they have a high value. Vase, $500; tumbler, $200. *Courtesy of Todd Baum and Jesse Speicher.*

Tumblers. Federal Glass Company. A box of 4.75" tall, 2.5" diameter tumblers was free with a purchase of Fleet-Wing gasoline. A bit of history helps to date this box. The Standard Oil Company was awarded the petroleum needs for the state of Ohio and opened their first gas station in 1913, acquiring Fleet-Wing Corporation of Cleveland, Ohio in the 1920s. Fleet-Wing was sold to Pennzoil in the late 1960s. Collectors of advertising, and those collecting gasoline-related memorabilia, will find this set particularly interesting. Tumblers, $8 each. Add $30 for box. *Courtesy Bill Phillips.*

Tumblers. Bartlett-Collins. These 3" tall, 2.5" diameter "Screen-decorated" tumblers from 1953 were created with a variety of stripes and animals along with other motifs. Values range from $5-$20 each depending on the decoration and color. Left to right, five examples in red are: one bunch of cherries, three bunches of cherries, cherries and roosters, four roosters, and three roosters. $7 each.

Tumblers. Unknown manufacturer. Little is know of these delicate "Thin Blown Tumblers" as even the original box offers nothing regarding their origin. $5 each. Add $20 for the original box. *Courtesy of Walt Lemiski – Waltz Time Antiques.*

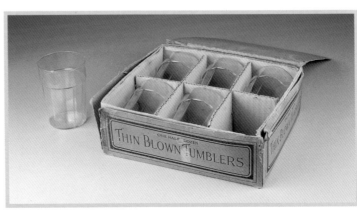

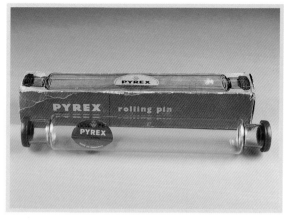

Rolling Pin. James A. Jobling & Co. Ltd., Wear Glass Works, Sunderland, England. The box provides directions and manufacturing information: "Fill with cold water or crushed ice for perfect pastry. Smooth, hard surface – easy to clean, never gets clogged with stale dough, 14" James A. Jobling & Co. Ltd. Wear Glass Works Sunderland England." This was obviously made for PYREX® by this British company. $85. Add $40 for original box. *Courtesy of David Mitchell.*

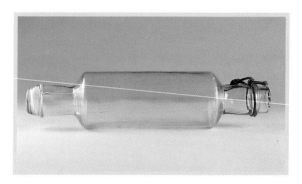

Rolling pin. Unknown manufacturer. The cork stopper is missing from a 14" rolling pin. $18 as shown without the stopper. *Courtesy of Walt Lemiski – Waltz Time Antiques.*

Tumblers. Hazel-Atlas Glass Company. Eight 5" tumblers looking much like Peanut Butter Glasses were sold together. One must presume that this was Hazel-Atlas' attempt to complete against floral tumblers that were "free" with the purchase of Boscul Peanut Butter in the 1950s. (For more information see *Peanut Butter Glasses, 2nd ed.* by Barbara.) Tumblers, $8 each. Add $20 for the original package. *Courtesy of Cheryl Kevish.*

Straw holders. Unknown manufacturers. Prized among kitchen glassware collectors, straw holders are being reproduced, and in fact sold for as little as $5 each in retail superstores. Take care before making a purchase; we recommend that you deal directly with a knowledgeable glass dealer. $125 each. *Courtesy of Walt Lemiski – Waltz Time Antiques.*

Mixer. Bentley-Beale, Inc., Montgomery, AL. The 12.5" tall "AIR-O-MIXER" is marked "PAT. APL'D. FOR MFG'D. BY BENTLEY-BEALE INC. MONTGOMERY, ALA. EGG BEATER DRINK MIXER CREAM WHIPPER MAYONNAISE MIXER." Pints, cups, and ounces are marked on the other side of the glass receptacle. $50.

Beverage Mixer. Silex. The twenty-four ounce, 9.25" tall (with stopper) container is designed "for MIXING AERATING and REFRIGERATOR STORAGE." Because it is made using tempered PYREX® glass it can store hot or cold liquids. $20. Add $20 for original packaging. *Courtesy of David Mitchell.*

Whip, mixer, and chopper jars. Dominion Glass Company and unknown manufacturers. Left to right: The whip with a green wooden knob has a glass base about 6" deep and almost 3" in diameter. The bottom is marked, "TODDY A MEAL IN A GLASS" and the lid is marked, "TODDY MIXER TAKES TEN SECONDS." The mixer with the metal handle has a glass base about 5.5" deep and 3" in diameter. It has no manufacturer's information of any kind. The taller red-knobbed chopper jar has a base that is 4.25" deep and 3.5" in diameter with no manufacturer's information. The red-knobbed chopper jar on the right is a Dominion Glass Company product with a base that is 3.5" deep and almost 3" in diameter. There are increments for quarter- and third-cups as well as lines for every two ounces. Left to right: $20, $20, $15, $15. *Courtesy of Walt Lemiski – Waltz Time Antiques.*

Whips. Androck and unknown manufacturers. The left and middle whips have no manufacturer's information of any kind. The whip on the right is marked, "ANDROCK PAT PENDING CAP'Y 14 OZ MADE IN USA." $45 each. *Courtesy of Walt Lemiski – Waltz Time Antiques.*

Beater jar. McKee Glass Company. Glasbake was a McKee line of ovenware. Deco lines add interest to a 5.25" deep, 4.5" diameter base that is marked, "4 34-113-A." The beater top is marked A&J. $50. *Courtesy of Walt Lemiski – Waltz Time Antiques.*

Bottle. Unknown manufacturer. Made for General Foods Corporation, this juice bottle has a 1954 copyright and was probably free with a General Foods purchase. One side of the bottle is marked "LEMONADE 32 OZ." and the other side is "ORANGE JUICE 24 OZ. 18 OZ. 12 OZ. 6 OZ. $25.

Recipes are found on the cap that covers the built-in strainer.

Cocktail shaker. Medco. The plastic lid of this 12.5" tall cocktail shaker includes beverage recipes on a turning dial. The base is marked, "MEDCO – 550 2 N.Y.C." $40. *Courtesy of Barbara Quick and Milton Quick.*

Mug. Unknown manufacturer. Federal Glass, Libbey, and other companies produced crystal barware with pink elephant decorations. This particular mug is 5" tall with a 3" diameter. $30. *Courtesy of Jan Wright.*

Cocktail shaker and tumbler. Unknown manufacturer. Federal Glass, Libbey, and other companies produced crystal barware with pink elephant decorations. Cocktail shakers are among the most collectible of all pink elephant glassware. Shaker, $100; tumbler, $15. *Courtesy of Carol Korn.*

Tumblers. Unknown manufacturer. Federal Glass, Libbey, and other companies produced crystal barware with pink elephant decorations. Shown are a variety of sizes, shapes, and elephant motifs. Note that the heavy-bottomed tumbler in this grouping has a different decoration than the heavy bottomed tumbler pictured with the pink elephant cocktail shaker. From largest to smallest the measurements are as follows: 6" tall, 2.5" diameter; 3.75" tall, almost 2.25" diameter; 3.25" tall, just over 3.25" diameter; 3.25" tall, just over 2.75" diameter; 2.75" tall, 2.75" diameter; 2.25" tall, almost 2" diameter. The smallest tumbler is a whiskey or shot glass that has "SAY WHEN" near the rim. $15 each. *Courtesy of Carol Korn.*

Ice bowl. Unknown manufacturer. 4.25" deep, 5.5" in diameter. *Courtesy of Carol Korn.*

Bowl. Jeannette Glass Company. Hand-painted Pennsylvania Dutch motifs decorate a 5" diameter, 3" deep mixing bowl. $25.

Close up of bottom mark. Many Jeannette Glass Company kitchenware items are unmarked.

Bowls. PYREX®. 1, 1-½, & 2-½-Quart Bowl Set, Item number 95 regularly sold for $5.96 but was offered for a special price of $4.44. Rolled edge PYREX® bowls are usually marked "SAFE FOR OVEN & MICROWAVE" making them more recent than many of the bowls featured in this book. $8 each bowl. Add $20 for original packaging as shown.

Knife. Dur-X. 8.5" in length, this is marked "MADE IN U.S.A." on one side and "DUR-X"" on the other. Dur-X Glass Fruit Knives were patented by John Didio of Buffalo, New York in November 1938. His sanitary approach to cutting and slicing acidic fruits (The box touted: This glass knife is specially made for oranges, lemons, grapefruit or limes – and no stain will show on the blade) was embraced by American homemakers and glass knives became a common-place tool. Knives were manufactured in lengths from 7.5" – 9.5" in crystal, as shown here, and in other transparent colors. $12. *Courtesy of Walt Lemiski – Waltz Time Antiques.*

Knife. Westmoreland Glass Company. 9" in length, the No. 1801 Fruit Knife design featured a guard to keep fingers from sliding forward during use. Add $30 for the box in good to excellent condition. $120. *Courtesy of Walt Lemiski – Waltz Time Antiques.*

DIRECTIONS: Use Glass Knife on soft wooden board only. Avoid using it on any metal or porcelain surface. To insure long use, keep the Glass Knife in its original box separate from your silverware. This Glass Knife cannot be exchanged for sanitary reasons.

Directions for use are provided on a side panel of the box.

Knife rest. A. H. Heisey & Company. An elaborate Corn Flower cut embellishes a 4" long knife rest. $60. *Courtesy of Walt Lemiski – Waltz Time Antiques.*

Spoons. Imperial Glass Company. These slightly blunt-tipped spoons are in the Candlewick pattern. The 4.75" long spoon has three ball of glass and the just-over 6" long spoon has two balls of glass. $20 each. *Courtesy of Walt Lemiski – Waltz Time Antiques.*

Ladles. Higbee Glass Company, The Cambridge Glass Company, and unknown manufacturers. Left to right: 6.5" long with a pouring lip in the 2.5" bowl; 6" long with a .75" rim and textured handle by Higbee – look for the bee mark; 5" long with a 1" rim; 5.5" long with a round bowl; 5" long with a round bowl. $10 each. *Courtesy of Walt Lemiski – Waltz Time Antiques.*

Funnels. Unknown manufacturers. Wide mouth funnels, like the one on the left, are extremely helpful when canning fruits and vegetables. It measures 4" in diameter at the top and 2" diameter at the base. The funnel on the right is just over 2.5" in diameter at the top and .25" in diameter at the base. Left, $12; right, $20. *Courtesy of Walt Lemiski – Waltz Time Antiques.*

Funnels. Mooney and unknown manufacturer. The 5.5" diameter funnel on the left is marked: "MOONEY AIRVENT 16 OZ." and the 6.75" diameter funnel on the right is marked "MADE IN U.S.A." Although not easily found in perfect condition, funnels are not in great demand at this time, particularly in crystal. $20 each. *Courtesy of Jack and Joyce Nichols.*

Salt box. Sneath Glass Company. The fine ribs separated by bands of glass explain the nickname "Triple Skip," which is found on other Sneath kitchen glass. This measures 3.5" in diameter and 3.5" deep and never had a lid. $40. *Courtesy of Tom Donlan.*

Salt dish and mug. Sneath Glass Company. The open salt never had a lid. It is 4" in diameter and 3.5" deep. The 5.25" tall mug is almost 3" in diameter. Salt, $40; mug, $25. *Courtesy of Walt Lemiski – Waltz Time Antiques.*

Cake pan. McKee Glass Company. Glasbake was a McKee line of ovenware. The apple-shaped cake pan is 10" x 9.75" x 1.5" deep. $15. *Courtesy of Walt Lemiski – Waltz Time Antiques.*

Casserole. McKee Glass Company. Glasbake was a McKee line of ovenware. Deco in style, the 8.5" diameter casserole has a base that is almost 4" deep. The bottom is marked: "QUEEN ANNE REG. U.S. PAT. OFF. GUARENTEED HEAT-RESISTING GLASBAKE." $40. *Courtesy of Walt Lemiski – Waltz Time Antiques.*

Skillet. Mary Dunbar. This 7" diameter, 1.25" deep all-glass skillet has a 4" handle and is marked "HEAT-FLOW Mary Dunbar TOP STOVE WATER PAT. U.S.A." $25. *Courtesy of Walt Lemiski – Waltz Time Antiques.*

Custard cups. PYREX®. Six 3.5" diameter, 2" deep custard cups are in the original wire rack. $5 each. Add $25 for the rack. *Courtesy of Walt Lemiski – Waltz Time Antiques.*

Water jar. Sneath Glass Company and McKee Glass Company. Although not often seen, water dispensers are not particularly popular with collectors, particularly in crystal (clear). The Sneath dispensers features vertical ribs and is actually more often seen in jade-ite than in crystal. The McKee dispenser was part of an entire line of glassware produced for storing foods and beverages. $150 each. *Courtesy of Walt Lemiski – Waltz Time Antiques.*

Washboard. Unknown manufacturer. The "MIDGET-WASHER" is 8.5" x 6". $85. *Courtesy of Walt Lemiski – Waltz Time Antiques.*

Food containers. Jewel Tea Co., Inc. "The Modern Way to Save and Preserve Foods" is with glass containers that went from the refrigerator to the pantry to the table. The Saverette included a ball-bearing lazy susan base for easy access to any of the five triangular containers. The value shown is for the set with the box and original documentation. Found individually, the glass containers would have little interest for most collectors. $85. *Courtesy of Walt Lemiski – Waltz Time Antiques.*

The Saverette package.

## Glass Containers

The containers are made under scientific manufacturing methods of clear, white, crystal, high quality glass with stippled decorations.

These closed glass containers protect, and preserve vitamin values in foods.

They're convenient—they eliminate handling jars, dishes, and pans of all sizes and shapes.

They're practical — the crystal glass containers show contents—do away with lifting of lids from pans and bowls to see contents.

They save space — they hold 20% more than other jars, dishes, or enameled-ware, used in the same amount of space.

### How to Use the Saverette
### in Refrigerator or Pantry

Place revolving tray on shelf where it is desired and insert glass containers in position on tray, one at a time. To select the container wanted, revolve tray with finger until the container required is before you; then grasp the container between the thumb and middle finger and lift out.

*TESTED AND APPROVED BY Mary Dunbar JEWEL HOMEMAKERS' INSTITUTE*

### Also endorsed by

Manufacturers of refrigerators, ice manufacturers, cooking schools, and teachers of Domestic Science, and by thousands of users.

**Manufactured for**

# JEWEL TEA CO., INC.
## JEWEL PARK, BARRINGTON, ILL.

*by Scurlock Kontanerette Corp., exclusive licensee*

# JEWEL FOOD SAVERETTE
### (Patents Pending)
### The "Last Word" in Food Containers

### The Modern Way to Save and Preserve Foods

In Refrigerators . . . Pantries . . . Kitchen Cabinets . . . also ideal for Buffet Luncheons (see inside page).

Contents always visible . . . in beautiful crystal glass containers.

It revolves on steel ball-bearings . . . "a flip of the finger" brings the container you want instantly.

They're economical . . . save space, food, money, and operating costs of refrigerators. . . . Permits you to buy large sized cans of food, thereby saving 10% to 20%.

# Every Home Should Use Two Saverettes
## One in the Refrigerator and Another in the Pantry

### Important Points to Remember

1. SANITARY — easy to clean. Closed glass containers protect the food.
2. ECONOMICAL — foods are sealed and keep fresh longer — a real saving.
3. CONVENIENT — "A FLIP OF THE FINGER" brings the container you want.
4. PRACTICAL — instant visibility, clear glass containers show contents plainly.
5. COMPACT — space saver — holds five quarts in 11½ inches of space—stores more food in less area.

To preserve vitamin values, keep all foods in closed kontaners.

### YOUR FRIEND WILL THANK YOU

Pass this on and tell her how she can get a JEWEL FOOD SAVERETTE--The "Last Word" in food containers---without cash outlay thru JEWEL SAVINGS. Recommend her to your Jewel man. He will be glad to offer her the same service he is giving you.

### Food Saverette For Luncheons

The Saverette is ideally adapted for card parties or afternoon luncheons, in that one may serve the hors-d'oeuvres and other afternoon delicacies in the most attractive manner.

The Saverette can be mounted on a Service Wagon, or placed on a small stand or table, and the hors-d'oeuvres, pickles, olives, cold meats, cheese, radishes, etc., can be placed in a container so that several kinds of food may be served. Revolving the tray, places before the guest the particular food desired. There's nothing today that equals the Saverette in attractiveness and convenience for this purpose.

Illustration shows pineapple, apricots, beets, pears and beans.

### "A Flip of the Finger" Brings the Container You Want

The brochure for the Savorette recommends owning two of these, one for the refrigerator and one for the pantry. Typical of Jewel Tea products, the brochure also encourages the buyer to refer a friend to her Jewel Tea man.

Jar. Sneath Glass Company. The Purity Oats jar was a premium offered with the purchase of said product. Made in the Colonial pattern, the 5.25" tall, 4.25" wide jar is embossed with an oat grain. The value of this jar is enhanced by having the original lid. $250 without lid, $450 with lid.

Jar. Unknown manufacturer. An interesting latching lid is on a 9.5" tall counter top jar. $85. *Courtesy of Walt Lemiski – Waltz Time Antiques.*

Canister and provisions jar. Unknown manufacturers. The canister is 6" tall and the provisions jar is 6.5" tall. The jade-ite colored silhouette décor, which is original and was used by Hall China, adds to the value of the jar. Canister, $15; jar, $40. *Courtesy of Walt Lemiski – Waltz Time Antiques.*

Canister. Owens-Illinois. Known as an "Ovide" canister because of the elliptical shape, this 8" tall canister retains an original label. The base is marked, "DES. PAT. 100014." $70. *Courtesy of Walt Lemiski – Waltz Time Antiques.*

Canister. Owens-Illinois. Known as an "Ovide" canister because of the elliptical shape, this 6.5" tall canister retains an original label. The base is marked, "DES. PAT. 100014." $70. *Courtesy of Tom Donlan.*

Jar. Owens-Illinois. Six center rings decorate a jar that originally contained Plee-zing Coffee from Chicago. When empty, a storage container was added to the kitchen. $50 as shown with label, $25 without label. *Courtesy of Tom Donlan.*

Jars. Jeannette Glass Company and unknown manufacturer. The 2.75" deep, 2.5" diameter condiment jar has a Jeannette mark on the base. The decorative cut is a Corn Flower look-alike. The 4.25" deep, 3" diameter provisions jar features vintage decorative decals. $14 each. *Courtesy of Walt Lemiski – Waltz Time Antiques.*

Shakers and canisters, presumed to be Hazel-Atlas. The graphics and decorations on these pieces are very similar to known Hazel-Atlas pieces leading one to consider Hazel-Atlas to be the manufacturer. The difference between a shaker and canister is simply the lid as shakers have holes for accessing the contents and canisters have solid lids for storing the contents. There are two sizes in this set: Nut-meats, Salt, Tea, Cocoa, and the Sugar on the right are 4.5" tall. Pepper, Sugar on the left, and Spices are 5" tall. Salt and pepper, $25 each; Sugar (either size), $35; Nut-meats, Tea, Cocoa, Spices, $45 each. *Courtesy of Fred MͨMorrow and Rodger Daye.b*

Canisters and shaker. Hazel-Atlas Glass Company. Known as "Fleur-de-lis" because of the black decoration below each name, this glassware comes in a variety of sizes, the smallest being shakers. Two textures are shown; the canister on the left has horizontal and vertical lines and the others have lines on a diagonal. The canisters are 7", just under 7", and 5", and the shakers are 4.5" tall. Canisters, $25 each; shakers, $15 each. *Courtesy of Walt Lemiski – Waltz Time Antiques.*

Shaker. Owens-Illinois. Known as an "Ovide" shaker because of the elliptical shape, this shaker retains an original label. $35. *Courtesy of Tom Donlan.*

Shaker. Unknown manufacturer. Measuring 3.75" tall, an unmarked sugar shaker features relief designs on all sides. $20. *Courtesy of Tom Donlan.*

Shaker. Owens-Illinois. Most common in Forest Green, this 4.25" tall shaker matches a set often referred to as "Rough and Ready." Original paper labels enhance value. Reproduction labels that are shiny with a foil-like border are being made. Shaker, $25 as shown with label, $15 without label. *Courtesy of Tom Donlan.*

John Mecroy and Son, Camden, New Jersey sold cinnamon in reusable Owens-Illinois shakers.

Shakers. Various manufacturers. Shown are five shakers, each with distinctive characteristics. Left to right: 4.5"
tall with no marks of any kind; 4.5" tall with "zipper" design and a base marked "NATIONAL GROCERS CO LTD"
indicating this may have been a premium offered through National Grocery Stores; 4.5" tall with a female figure
embossed in the glass and the Sellers mark on the base; two 4.75" tall shakers with worn original labels. Left to
right: $30, $30, $30, $15, $15. *Courtesy of Walt Lemiski – Waltz Time Antiques.*

Shakers. Anchor Hocking Glass Company. Striped shakers were sold in pairs and were made in black, blue, red,
green, and yellow. Two colors are pictured here. The clear shakers on the right have the "Tulip" lids that were
also used on Fire-King range sets. Often collectors purchase clear shakers as shown here and transfer the lids to
more valuable Fire-King shakers. $10 each. *Courtesy of Walt Lemiski – Waltz Time Antiques.*

Shaker: Unknown manufacturer. This 6" tall shaker features a lid that dispenses one tablespoon of sugar when tipped. The 3.75" diameter base retains its original rubber bumper designed to protect it from damage. This unusual shaker is shown assembled and unassembled. $85. *Courtesy of Walt Lemiski – Waltz Time Antiques.*

Syrup pitchers. Unknown manufacturers. 4.5" tall with a decorative cut and 5.75" tall. $25 each. *Courtesy of Walt Lemiski – Waltz Time Antiques.*

Jam jar and sugar box. U.S. Glass Company and unknown manufacturer. The 3" diameter, 3.5" deep jam jar is by U.S. Glass Company. The sugar box is 5" in diameter and 3" deep. $45 each. *Courtesy of Walt Lemiski – Waltz Time Antiques.*

Gravy boat and under plate. Unknown manufacturer. The 2.75" tall (at the handle) gravy boat has a 5.5" x 3.75" under plate. $40. *Courtesy of Walt Lemiski – Waltz Time Antiques.*

The Pot Watcher. Unknown manufacturer. Just over 3" in diameter, this is placed in a kettle of water and rattles from the movement of the bubbles when the water boils. $15, *Courtesy of Walt Lemiski – Waltz Time Antiques.*

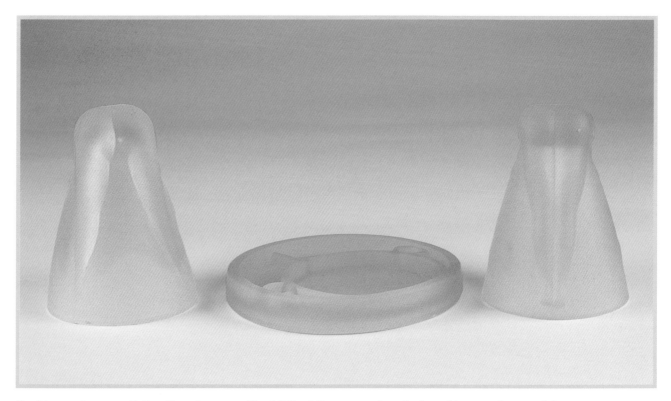

Tumblers and coaster. McKee Glass Company. The 3.25" tall "bottoms up" cocktail tumblers are shown with legs together and split; split legs are much more difficult to find. The coaster is 4" in diameter. Look for patent number 77725 on vintage tumblers. Tumbler with closed legs, $175; split, $275; coaster, $100. *Courtesy of Todd Baum and Jesse Speicher.*

Cruets. Heisey. An 8" tall "Plantation" cruet is next to a 4.5" tall "Pleat and Panel" cruet. Plantation, $85; Pleat and Panel, $50. *Courtesy of Walt Lemiski – Waltz Time Antiques.*

Ice cream dish. Unknown manufacturer. Designed to hold two scoops of ice cream, this is 3" tall and 4.75" wide.

Batter and syrup pitchers. The Washington Company. The 9.5" tall dispenser is for neatly pouring waffle batter, and the 5.5" tall dispenser is for the syrup. Hand-painted details enhance the value of this "batter set". Batter pitcher, $35; syrup pitcher, $30.

The original sticker remains on the batter dispenser and adds $10 to the value.

The batter and syrup pitchers were sold together. Add $20 for the box.

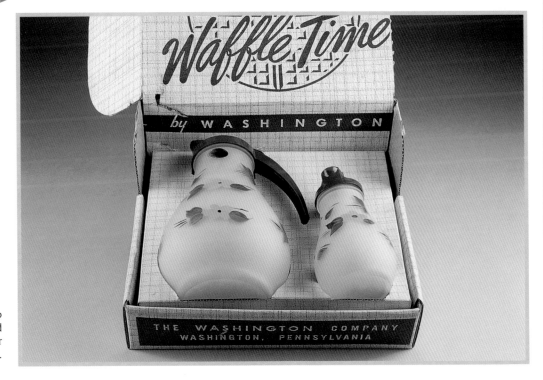

Batter and syrup pitchers. Unknown manufacturer. The 9.5" tall dispenser is for neatly pouring waffle batter, and the 5.5" tall dispenser is for the syrup. Hand-painted details enhance the value of each. Batter pitcher, $35; syrup pitcher, $30.

Canisters and shaker. Owens-Illinois. Most common in Forest Green, shown are pieces from a set often referred to as "Rough and Ready." The canisters are 7" tall and 5.25" tall and the shaker is 4.25" tall. Had they survived, original paper labels would have enhanced the values. Canisters, $40 each, shaker, $20. *Courtesy of Walt Lemiski – Waltz Time Antiques.*

Shakers. McKee Glass Company. 4.5" tall square shakers with lettering sometimes referred to as "Deco lettering." These shakers feature the smaller-size letters in a color McKee called "French Ivory." Salt, Pepper, Flour, $60 each; others, $75 each. *Courtesy of Todd Baum and Jesse Speicher.*

Shakers. McKee Glass Company. Large-size red "Deco lettering" on 4.5" tall shakers is much more difficult to find than black "Deco lettering" in either size. $90 each. *Courtesy of Todd Baum and Jesse Speicher.*

Shakers. McKee Glass Company. Large "Deco lettering" on 4.5" tall shakers. Salt, Pepper, Flour, $70 each; others, $85 each. *Courtesy of Walt Lemiski – Waltz Time Antiques.*

Shakers. Hocking Glass Company. Most shakers have horizontal lettering so when the alignment is vertical or on an angle the value of the shaker increases. These Pepper, Flour, and Sugar shakers were written in French for use in Quebec, Canada. $95 each. *Courtesy of Walt Lemiski – Waltz Time Antiques.*

Shaker. McKee Glass Company. Even with crisp lettering as shown, this shaker is valued significantly less that the other McKee examples due to the lack of color and additional details to the lettering. $25. *Courtesy of Tom Donlan.*

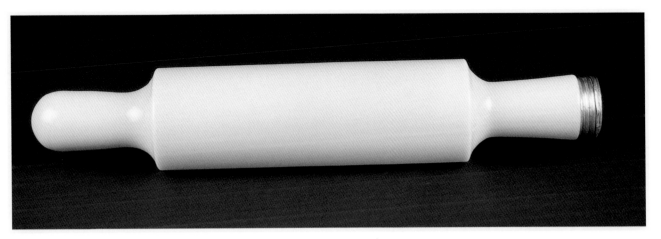

Rolling pin. McKee Glass Company. 16" long. $500.
*Courtesy of Todd Baum and Jesse Speicher.*

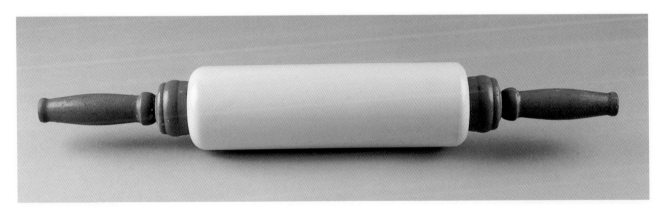

Rolling pin. Imperial Manufacturing Company. The 19" rolling pin features green wooden handles, making this no earlier than 1927, the year when colored handles were introduced. The end is embossed: PATENTED IMPERIAL MFG. CO. CAMBRIDGE OHIO U.S.A." $500.
*Courtesy of Aniceta Zamborsky.*

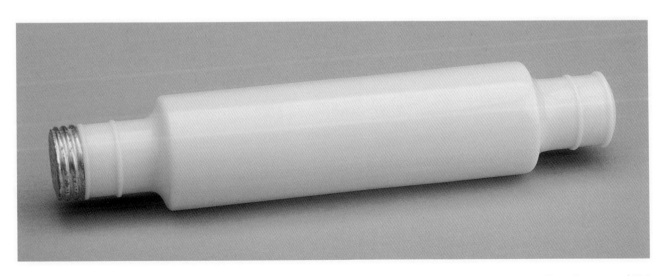

Rolling pin. McKee Glass Company. $500.
*Courtesy of Tom Donlan.*

Butter dishes. McKee Glass Company. Left: The "Covered Butter Box" which originally sold for fifty cents has the following measurements: base: 8.5" handle to handle x 4"; cover: 7" x 3.25" x 2.5" deep. Right: A green stripe greatly enhances the value of this butter dish that has the following measurements: base: 6.5" handle to handle x 3.5"; cover: 6" x 3.5" x 2.5" deep. Look for the daisy-like motif on McKee butter covers. Left, $100; right: $150. *Courtesy of Todd Baum and Jesse Speicher.*

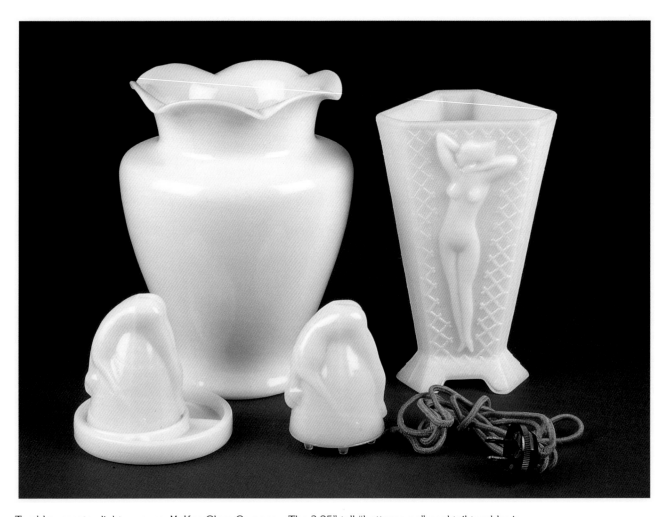

Tumbler, coaster, lighter, vases. McKee Glass Company. The 3.25" tall "bottoms up" cocktail tumbler is on the 4" coaster. Look for patent number 77725 on vintage bottoms up tumblers. The lighter, which is fashioned from the cocktail tumbler, is quite rare. The 8" tall Sarah vase is next to a 7.5" tall No. 100 nude "Triangle" vase. Tumbler, $150; coaster, $150; lighter, $250; Sarah vase, $100; nude vase, $350. *Courtesy of Todd Baum and Jesse Speicher.*

 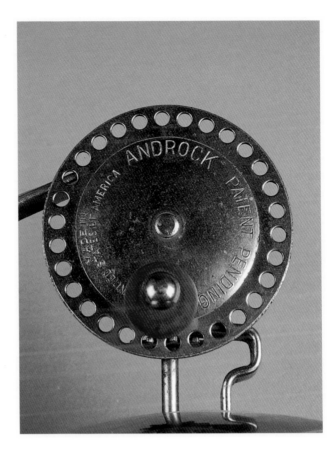

Whip. McKee Glass Company. An Androck mechanism is made to fit a 4" diameter, 2.75" deep, lipped bowl. $80. *Courtesy of Todd Baum and Jesse Speicher.*

Underside of the lighter.

Cheese dish. McKee Glass Company. Part of the "Laurel" dinnerware collection, the base is a 7.5" plate and the lid is 5.25" in diameter and about 2.5" along the side. $100. *Courtesy of Walt Lemiski – Waltz Time Antiques.*

# Fired-On Colors — Blue

Vase. Anchor Hocking Glass Company. Measuring 3.75" in height and 4" in diameter, this vase is often referred to as a "Squatty" vase. $15.

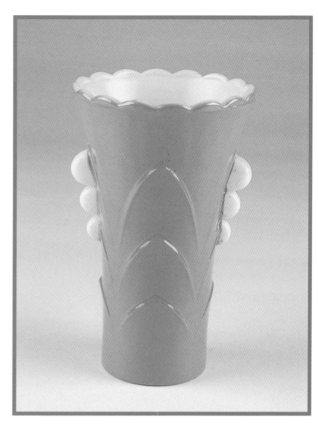

Vase. Fire-King by Anchor Hocking Glass Company. 5.25" tall Deco vases were produced in an array of colors, and shown is a vase that is white with blue applied to, or fired onto, the outside $35. *Courtesy of Todd Baum and Jesse Speicher.*

Cup. McKee Glass Company. Glasbake was a McKee line of ovenware. The square cup pictured here was made in various pastel hues. $5. *Courtesy of Linda and Ron Peterson.*

Shaker. Hazel-Atlas. 4.5" tall. $65.

Oil-vinegar bottle. Gemco. A 6" tall oil bottle – used for oil and vinegar – is marked "W4 gemco U.S.A." and can be found in a variety of colors often retaining the original label. $10. *Courtesy of Walt Lemiski – Waltz Time Antiques.*

Bowls. PYREX®. Marked "FOR OVEN & MICROWAVE," these bowls are also sized: 1 L, 1.5 L, and 2.5 L, and measure 7" in diameter, 3" deep; 8.5" in diameter, 3.5" deep; 10" in diameter, 4" deep. $15 each.

Bowls. Fire-King by Anchor Hocking Glass Company. This set was placed with the blue fired-on glass because the largest bowl is blue. Measurements are as follows: blue: 10" handle to handle, 8.75" diameter, 4.25" deep; yellow: 8.5" handle to handle, 7.25" diameter, 4" deep; red: 7" handle to handle, 6" diameter, 3.75" deep. $14 each.

Pitcher and tumbler. Hocking Glass Company and Hazel-Atlas Glass Company. The tilt pitcher is from the "Rainbow" line of colorful fired-on Hocking glassware and the 4.5" tall, 2.5" diameter tumbler is by Hazel-Atlas. Pitcher, $75; tumbler, $12.

# Fired-On Colors — Gray

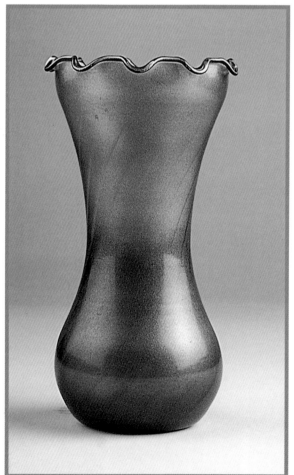

Vase. Anchor Hocking Glass Company. Gray is an uncommon color and most likely from the 1950s. This 6.75" tall vase was molded with a subtle spiral optic and a ruffled rim. $15.

Canisters. Hazel-Atlas Glass Company. Flour, 7.5"
tall; Sugar, 6.5" tall; Coffee, 6.5" tall; Tea, 5" tall.
Left to right: $125, $100, $100, $85. *Courtesy of
Todd Baum and Jesse Speicher.*

Shaker. Hazel-Atlas Glass Company.
4.5" tall; a matching pepper shaker
is available. $100 each. *Courtesy of
Todd Baum and Jesse Speicher.*

Shakers. Hocking Glass Company. Waterford Depression Glass is the inspiration for these shakers. $25.

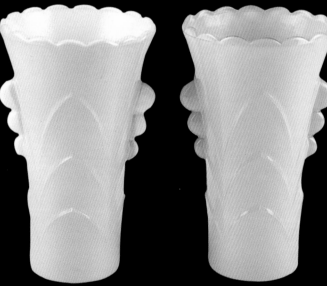

Vase. Anchor Hocking Glass Company. A 9" tall "Hoover" vase features hand-painted embellishments. $20.

Vases. Fire-King by Anchor Hocking Glass Company. The 5.25" tall Deco vases were produced in an array of colors, and shown are two fired-on green vases. The vase on the left is white with green applied on the outside while the vase on the right is clear with green applied to the outside. Collectors seem to prefer the "finished" look of a white interior. Left, $35; right, $28. *Courtesy of Todd Baum and Jesse Speicher.*

Cup. McKee Glass Company. Glasbake was a McKee line of ovenware. The square cup pictured here was made in various pastel hues. $5. *Courtesy of Linda and Ron Peterson.*

Candlesticks. Unknown manufacturer. Silver embellishments enhance a pair of candlesticks that match Jade-ite glassware. $20 each.

The manufacturer's sticker.

Pitcher. Anchor Hocking Glass Company. Fired-on glassware is rarely as decorative as this 4.75" tall pitcher, probably used for cream or milk. $40. Add $10 for an original sticker. *Courtesy of Gary and Donna Kovar.*

Bowls. Hocking Glass Company. These bowls are a perfect match for actual jade-ite glassware. The dimensions, from largest to smallest follow: 10.5" diameter, 4.75" deep; 9.5" diameter, 4.5" deep; 8.75" diameter, 4" deep; 7.75" diameter, 3.75" deep. $30 each. *Courtesy of Ron and Sue Dibeler.*

Drink dispenser. Unknown manufacturer. Created for commercial use, the base of this dispenser is fired-on green. $300. *Courtesy of Terry and Don Yusko.*

Bowl and pitcher. Hocking Glass Company. The bowl is 8.5" in diameter (10.25" handle to handle) and 3" deep. The tilt pitcher is 6.5" tall at the handle. Bowl, $18; pitcher, $35. *Courtesy of Walt Lemiski – Waltz Time Antiques.*

Vase. Fire-King by Anchor Hocking Glass Company. The 5.25" tall Deco vases were produced in an array of colors. $30. *Courtesy of Todd Baum and Jesse Speicher.*

Vase. Anchor Hocking Glass Company. The 8.75" tall "Pineapple Vase" was made in transparent pink and various fired-on colors. $25.

Sugar box and shaker. Medco and Hazel-Atlas Glass Company. The 3" deep, 4.5" diameter sugar or salt box is marked "MADE IN U.S.A. MEDCO N.Y.C." The 4.5" tall shaker is often referred to as a "barrel shaker." $40 each.

Vase. Fire-King by Anchor Hocking
Glass Company. 5.25" tall Deco
vases were produced in an array of
colors, and shown is a vase that is
white with pink applied on the
outside $25. *Courtesy of Todd Baum
and Jesse Speicher.*

Pitcher. Hocking Glass
Company. Measuring
5.5" tall at the handle,
the applied color is a
deep rose. $75.

Cup. McKee Glass Company. Glasbake was a McKee line of ovenware. The square cup pictured here was made in various pastel hues. $5. *Courtesy of Linda and Ron Peterson.*

The Glasbake name is embossed on the bottom of most of their pieces.

Apothecary jar. Anchor Hocking Glass Company. This 8.25" tall jar may have been sold with soap or a similar bath item inside. $25.

Refrigerator dish and bowl. Hocking Glass Company. From 1932, these fired-on items retain great color. The refrigerator dish is 5.75" x 3.5" x 2" deep and the mixing bowl is 8.25" in diameter and 3.25" deep. $35 each. *Courtesy of Walt Lemiski – Waltz Time Antiques.*

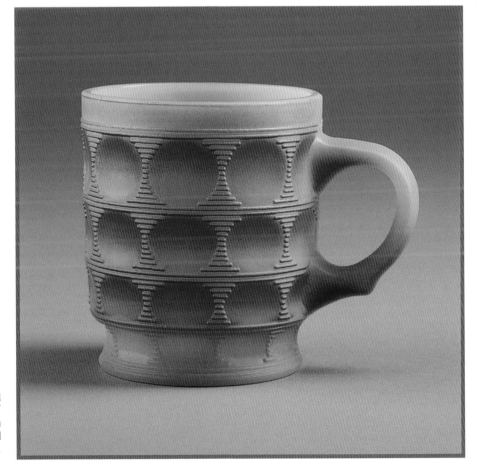

Mug. Fire-King by Anchor Hocking Glass Company. An unusual 3.5" tall, 3" diameter mug features a Deco design highlighted with red and green fired-on colors. $25.

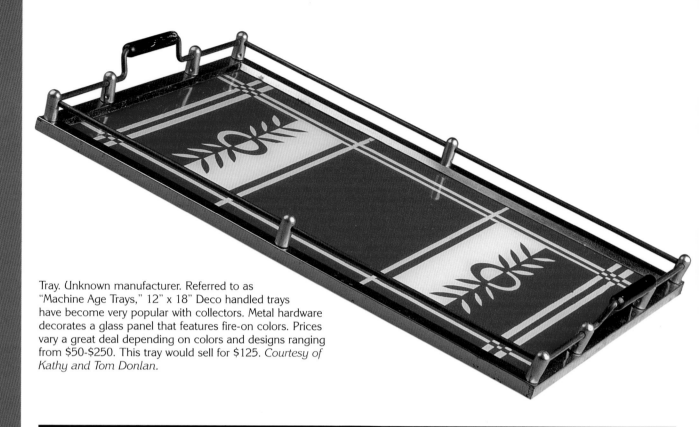

Tray. Unknown manufacturer. Referred to as "Machine Age Trays," 12" x 18" Deco handled trays have become very popular with collectors. Metal hardware decorates a glass panel that features fire-on colors. Prices vary a great deal depending on colors and designs ranging from $50-$250. This tray would sell for $125. *Courtesy of Kathy and Tom Donlan.*

# Fired-On Colors – White

Oil-vinegar bottle. Gemco. This 6" tall oil bottle – used for oil and vinegar – is marked "gemco U.S.A." and can be found in a variety of colors often retaining the original label. $10. *Courtesy of Walt Lemiski – Waltz Time Antiques.*

Pitcher. Bartlett-Collins Company. Many hand-painted pitchers and tumblers have been incorrectly attributed to Hocking Glass Company. One way to easily distinguish glassware between these two manufacturers is to note the smooth "throat" of this pitcher, a Bartlett-Collins characteristic, while Hocking pitchers are ribbed at the throat. Matching tumblers were made in this grape motif. The pitcher is 9" tall at the handle. Pitcher, $20; tumbler (not pictured), $5. *Courtesy of Jack and Joyce Nichols.*

Cup. McKee Glass Company. Glasbake was a McKee line of ovenware. The square cup pictured here was made in various pastel hues. $5. *Courtesy of Linda and Ron Peterson.*

Flower pots. Hocking Glass Company. The 2.25" square flower pot is 2.5" deep with four feet. The 2.25" diameter round flower pot is 2.25" deep and reminiscent of the Colonial "Knife and Fork" Depression Glass dinnerware pattern. $12 each. *Courtesy of Walt Lemiski – Waltz Time Antiques.*

Vase. Anchor Hocking Glass Company. This 8.75" tall "Pineapple Vase" was made in transparent pink and various fired-on colors. $25.

Vase. Hocking Glass Company. 3.75" tall, 4" opening. $18.

# Green
# — Forest and Other Dark Transparent Hues

Napkin holder. NAPCO. "NAPCO 1164 CLEVELAND.O. U.S.A" is the marking found on the base of this napkin holder. $100. *Courtesy of Walt Lemiski – Waltz Time Antiques.*

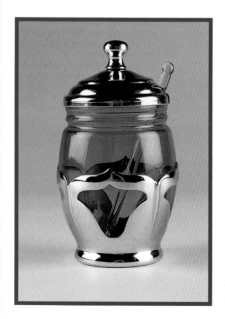

Condiment jar. Farber Brothers. A 3.5" tall, 2.25" diameter base is encapsulated in Farber Brothers chrome which is marked: "FARBER BROS NEW YORK, N.Y. PAT. AUG 2nd 1932." A 4" long crystal (clear) spoon neatly fits through the notched chrome lid. $65. *Courtesy of Walt Lemiski – Waltz Time Antiques.*

Relish. Unknown manufacturer. The 10" diameter, five-part relish has a 1" rim. $45. *Courtesy of Walt Lemiski – Waltz Time Antiques.*

Canisters. Owens-Illinois. 8" tall "Rough and Ready" canisters have original paper labels written in French for use in Quebec, Canada. Americans view these as unique and place a higher value on them than do French Canadians. $85 each. *Courtesy of Walt Lemiski – Waltz Time Antiques.*

Shakers. Owens-Illinois. The 4.5" tall "Rough and Ready" pepper shaker retains part of an original label. Matching canisters in two sizes are available. The vertically ribbed shaker is 4.25" tall. The 3.5" tall shaker features a Bakelite lid with the Owen-Illinois logo molded into it. Original paper labels will enhance the values. Left and middle, $20 each; right, $35 because of the lid. *Courtesy of Walt Lemiski – Waltz Time Antiques.*

The Owens-Illinois symbol is common on their glassware but rare on a lid as shown here. *Courtesy of Walt Lemiski – Waltz Time Antiques.*

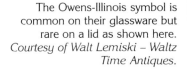

Provisions jar. Thought to be Hocking Glass Company. Much of the Forest Green glassware was produced by Hocking Glass Company and Owens-Illinois, companies that usually mark their products, but this jar has no manufacturer's information. Common in crystal (clear) and often seen in transparent green, a Forest Green jar is rare. $175. *Courtesy of Walt Lemiski – Waltz Time Antiques.*

Bottles. Owens-Illinois. The 9.95" tall bottle on the left and the 8.75" tall bottle in the middle feature the same waterfall motif. The 8.75" bottle on the right features a wishing well. The capacity of the bottles is molded into the back of each as either "2QTS" or "1QT." $45 each. *Courtesy of Walt Lemiski – Waltz Time Antiques.*

Bottle. Owens-Illinois. The cap on this 6.75" tall bottle is quite interesting as it features a built-in strainer. $45. *Courtesy of Dennis A. Busold, Robin's Nest Antiques.*

An underside view of the cap shows the straining feature of this clever lid.

Syrup pitcher. Paden City Glass Manufacturing Company. Measuring slightly less than 4" tall, there is a metal under plate available for this item. The cuts in this Emerald-Glo pitcher are distinctive characteristics of Paden City glassware. $55. *Courtesy of The Attic Annex, Joyce and Jim Coverston.*

Refrigerator dish. Unknown manufacturer. The lid of this 8" x 12" refrigerator dish is embossed with its purpose: "VEGETABLE FRESHENER." $85. *Courtesy of Dennis A. Busold, Robin's Nest Antiques.*

Vase. McKee Glass Company. The "Modern Square" design is on this 7.75" tall, 7.75" diameter vase. $450. *Courtesy of Todd Baum and Jesse Speicher.*

Vases. McKee Glass Company. Three different shades of green are seen on these 8.5" tall No. 100 nude "Triangle" vases. $200 each. *Courtesy of Todd Baum and Jesse Speicher.*

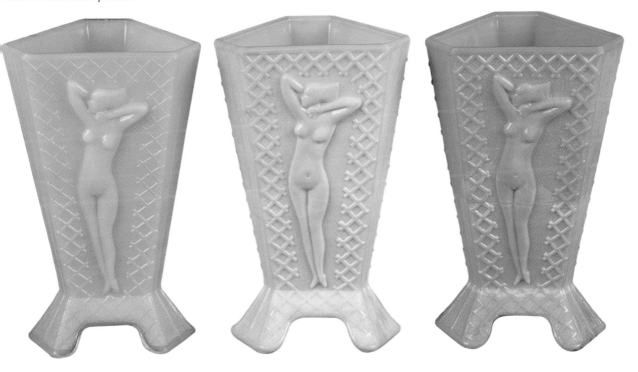

Vase. McKee Glass Company. This 7.5"
"Triangle" vase is in an unusual shade of
jade-ite. $250. Courtesy of Todd Baum
and Jesse Speicher.

Vase and candy jar. McKee Glass Company. The dressed figure on the 8.5"
tall "Triangle" vase is more difficult to find than a nude one. When a lid is
place on the 7.5" tall vase it becomes a candy jar. Dressed vase, $275;
7.5" base, $200; lid, $225. *Courtesy of Todd Baum and Jesse Speicher.*

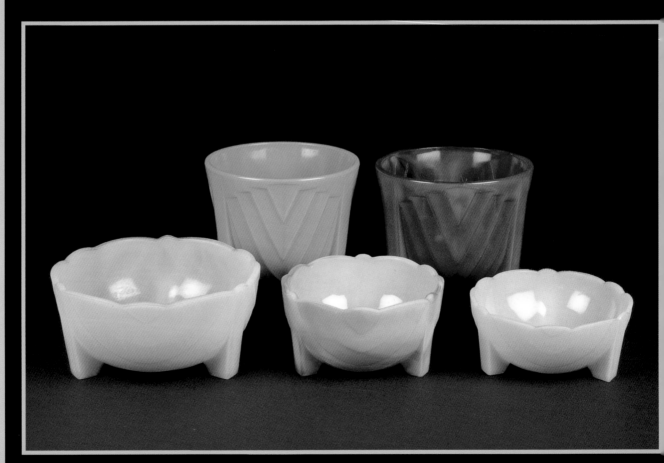

Jardinières and bulb bowls. McKee Glass Company. Back row: two 6" diameter, 5.5" deep, three-footed No. 25
jardinières; front row: three different bulb bowls measuring 7" diameter, 3.25" deep; 5.5" diameter, 2.75" deep;
and 5.5" diameter, 2.5" deep. These were introduced in 1931. $125 each. *Courtesy of Todd Baum and Jesse*

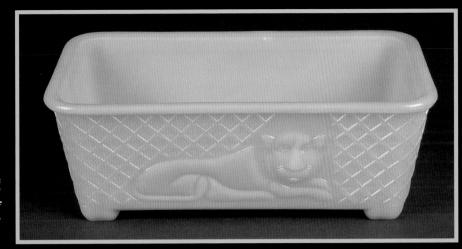

Window box planter. McKee Glass Company. 5" x 9" x 3" deep. $125. *Courtesy of Todd Baum and Jesse Speicher.*

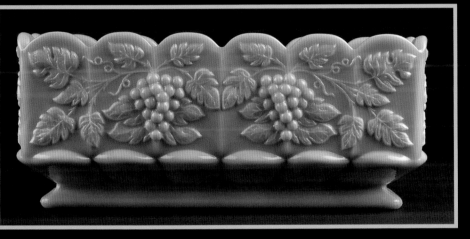

Window box planter. Thought to be Westmoreland. The "Beaded Grape" motif is highly dimensional on this 8.5" x 4" x 3.5" deep planter. We have a company listing of the pieces made in Pattern #1884 – Beaded Grape, and this window box planter is not included, so we cannot be certain that this a true Beaded Grape piece. $150. *Courtesy of Faye and Robert Smith.*

Cookie jar. McKee Glass Company. The 5.25" tall, 6" in diameter, No. 25 three-footed jardinière became a cookie jar with addition of a lid. Base, $125; lid, $175. *Courtesy of Todd Baum and Jesse Speicher.*

Mixmaster. Sunbeam. Jeannette Glass Company is thought to have provided much of the jade-ite used to accompany these still-popular appliances, $150. *Courtesy of Walt Lemiski – Waltz Time Antiques.*

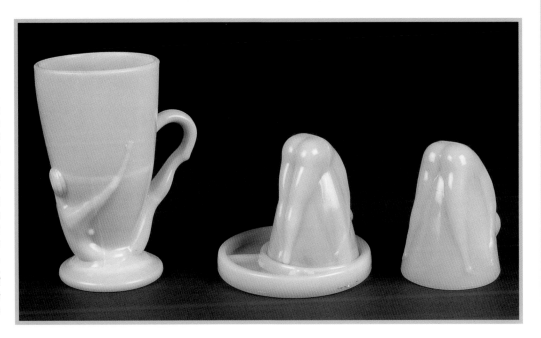

Tumblers, coaster, and mug. McKee Glass Company. The 3.25" tall "bottoms up" cocktail tumblers are shown with legs together and split; split legs are much more difficult to find. The coaster is 4" in diameter. The "bottoms down" mug is 5.5" tall. Look for patent number 77725 on vintage tumblers and mugs. Tumbler with closed legs, $175; split, $275; coaster, $100; mug, $350. *Courtesy of Todd Baum and Jesse Speicher.*

Ashtray. Unknown manufacturer. European in origin, this 4.5" diameter ashtray has no markings. $30. *Courtesy of Walt Lemiski – Waltz Time Antiques.*

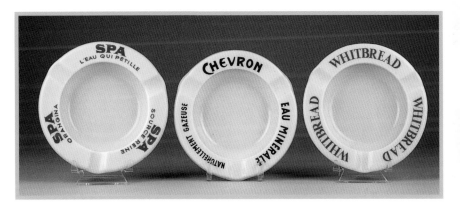

Ashtrays. Unknown manufacturers. European in origin, these advertising ashtrays have no markings but certainly appear to have been made by the same company. They are almost 6" in diameter. $45 each. *Courtesy of Walt Lemiski – Waltz Time Antiques.*

Cheese dish. McKee Glass Company. Part of the "Laurel" dinnerware collection made in the 1930s, the base is a 7.5" plate and the lid is 5.25" in diameter and about 2.5" high. $375. *Courtesy of Walt Lemiski – Waltz Time Antiques.*

Custard cups. Glasbake, McKee Glass Company, Fire-King by Anchor Hocking Glass Company. Left to right: 2.25" deep with 2.75" diameter and Philbe-like embellishments, marked "Glasbake"; 2.25" deep with 2.75" diameter, marked "McK"; 2.5" deep with 3" diameter, marked "Fire-King OVEN WARE." $85 each.

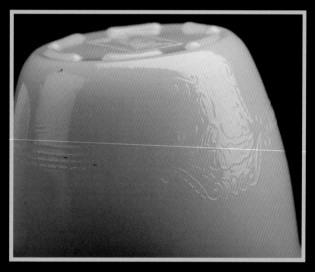

This view shows the feet and Philbe-like design of the Glasbake custard cup shown on the left.

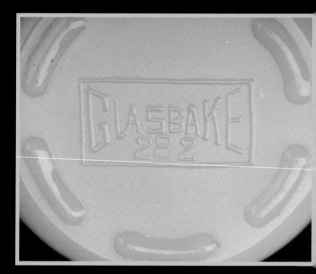

The mark on the bottom of the Glasbake custard cup.

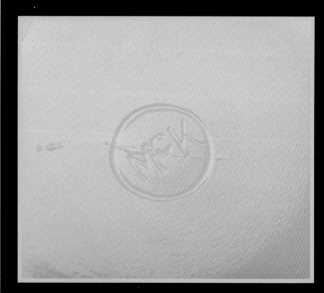

McK is the mark found on most McKee Glass Company

The Fire-King custard cup on the right is clearly marked.

Shakers. Jeannette Glass Company. Many pieces of jade-ite kitchen glass can be found in light and dark tones. Collectors usually prefer the darker pieces as they are less common. The same 4.75" tall shakers clearly show different coloration. Dark, $250; light, $175. *Courtesy of Linda and Ron Peterson.*

Canister. McKee Glass Company. This design is referred to as a "Column Canister." Shown is the 7.75" size that has a diameter of 4". $1000+. *Courtesy of Linda and Ron Peterson.*

Decanter and bottle. McKee Glass Company. The "pinched" design allowed for ease in use of the decanter and water bottle. $250 each. *Courtesy of John and Marilyn Yallop.*

Bowl. McKee Glass Company. Decorative bowls are not often seen; most Jade-ite glassware was purely utilitarian. $250. *Courtesy of John and Marilyn Yallop.*

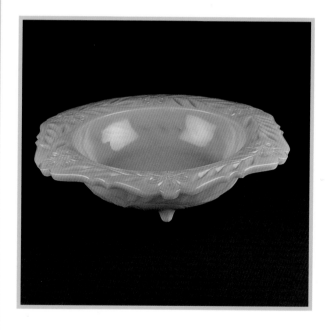

Bowl. McKee Glass Company. Decorative bowls are not often seen; most Jade-ite glassware was purely utilitarian. $250. *Courtesy of John and Marilyn Yallop.*

Bowl and candleholders. McKee Glass Company. Two 4" candleholders with a matching 8.5" bowl were sold as a console set in this Autumn pattern from 1934. Bowl, $200; candleholders, $75 each. *Courtesy of John and Marilyn Yallop.*

Ladle. Cambridge Glass Company. Opalescent Jade-ite is not commonly seen, adding to the allure of this 5" long, flat-bottomed ladle. $75. *Courtesy of Carol Korn.*

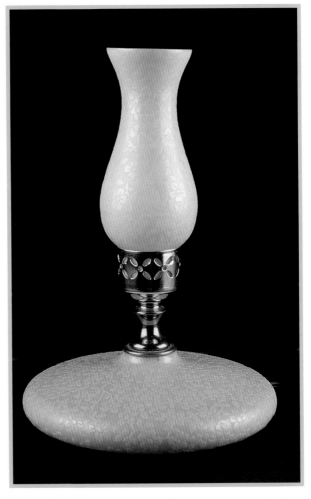

Bowl. McKee Glass Company. This opalescent bowl is 6" in diameter when measured handle to handle or 4.25" in diameter and 2.5" deep. The opalescence adds to its beauty and uniqueness. $175. *Courtesy of Keith and Judy Hendrix.*

Lamp. Unknown manufacturer. Although not a true kitchen item, this is worth one's attention. The all-over floral motif is quite lovely and truly unique. $300. *Courtesy of John and Marilyn Yallop.*

# Green —
# Transparent

Shakers. Hazel-Atlas Glass Company. These G-1491 shakers were only made in these four variations. 4.5" shakers such as these are range sets for use while cooking. Care must be taken when selecting shakers for purchase as they have been reproduced. $85 each. *Courtesy of Clark Crawford.*

Shaker. Hazel-Atlas Glass Company. 5" tall. $20. *Courtesy of Walt Lemiski – Waltz Time Antiques.*

Shakers. Hazel-Atlas Glass Company and unknown manufacturer. Measurements were taken to the top of the lids. Left to right: unknown manufacturer, 3.25" tall; middle: Hazel-Atlas from the late 1920s-early 1930s, 3.75" tall; right: made by Hazel-Atlas and sometimes referred to as "X Design," 3.5" tall. $45 per pair.

Sugar dispenser. U.S. Glass Company. 5.25" tall with 3.5" diameter at base. $125. *Courtesy of Walt Lemiski – Waltz Time Antiques.*

Napkin holder and sugar dispenser. Paden City Glass Manufacturing Company and unknown manufacturer. The napkin holder is part of Paden City's Party Line and is 4" tall x 2.25" wide x 3.25" deep. The 5.5" tall dispenser features a paneled optic and cinched design for ease in use. Napkin holder, $275; sugar dispenser, $275. *Courtesy of Russ and Ann Dippon.*

Sugar dispenser. Unknown manufacturer. The base of this 6.25" tall pourer is marked "PAT. APPLD FOR." $225. *Courtesy of Charles and Susan Keye.*

Canister and provisions jar. Hazel-Atlas Glass Company. The canister is 6" tall and 3.75" wide. The small provisions jar has a 3.5" deep base and the opening is just over 2". Canister, $185, provisions jar, $50. *Courtesy of Russ and Ann Dippon.*

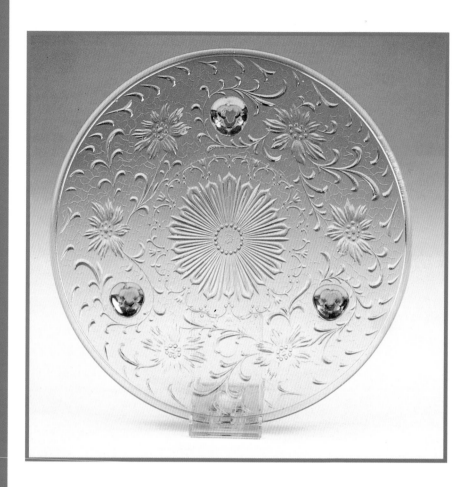

Cake plate. U.S. Glass Company. Nicknamed "Shaggy Daisy" by Hazel Marie Weatherman, this three-footed cake plate was also used to cover mixing bowls thus allowing one to use them as refrigerator dishes. $35.

Cake plate. U.S. Glass Company. Nicknamed "Rose Burr" by Hazel Marie Weatherman, this three-footed, 9.5" diameter cake plate was also used to cover mixing bowls, thus allowing one to use them as refrigerator dishes. $35. *Courtesy of Clark Crawford.*

Trivet. U.S. Glass Company. Nicknamed "Wallflower" by Hazel Marie Weatherman, this 5.5" diameter utility plate was also used to cover mixing bowls, thus converting their use to refrigerator dishes. $35.

Bowls. Hazel-Atlas Glass Company. Shown are two bowls from a set that is known to have four. The design, which incorporates a spout, allows for ease in pouring batter, hence this style is often called a "batter bowl." Company catalogues listed them as "Mixing Bowl with Lip." $40 each. *Courtesy of Clark Crawford.*

Bowls. Hazel-Atlas Glass Company. Introduced in 1929, these smooth bowls were made in 4, 5, 6, and 7-inch diameters. $20 each.

Bowl and plate. U.S. Glass Company. The 8.25" diameter, 4.5" deep batter bowl is marked; "D & B Co." The 9" diameter plate, which measures 10" from handle to handle, fits on top as a lid. This bowl style has been nicknamed "Stick." It is interesting to note that the manufacturer sold this bowl in a set of five and only the largest one, which is shown here, was handled. The handled bowl was also offered as part of a kitchen set that included a reamer and measuring cup combination and three covered refrigerator dishes. Company catalogues show three bowls with three glass "lids" as shown here offered together as the "No. 8135 Six-Piece Refrigerator Set." Batter bowl, $50; plate, $25. *Courtesy of Walt Lemiski – Waltz Time Antiques.*

Cake plate and bowl. U.S. Glass Company. Nicknamed "Rose Burr" by Hazel Marie Weatherman, this three-footed, 9.5" diameter cake plate is being used to cover a mixing bowl, thus allowing one to use it as a refrigerator dish. Company catalogues do not show this decorative cake plate for sale with mixing bowls; they were efficiently and effectively designed for multipurpose use and sold separately. Cake plate, $35; bowl, $25.

Bowls and measuring cups. U.S. Glass Company. Two "Stick" batter bowls are shown with one-cup measures: note the variations in color. Bowls, $50 each; measuring cups $70 each. *Courtesy of Clark Crawford.*

An advertisement at the bottom of the measuring cup on the right indicates that it was probably given away free. *Courtesy of Clark Crawford.*

Measuring cup. Unknown manufacturer. Increments for ounces, ¼-cup, and ⅓-cup are shown in a 2.75" deep one-cup measure. This unusual design has the full one-cup mark quite close to the rim, indicating an early design as later measures were developed to be more user-friendly. $85. *Courtesy of Carol Korn.*

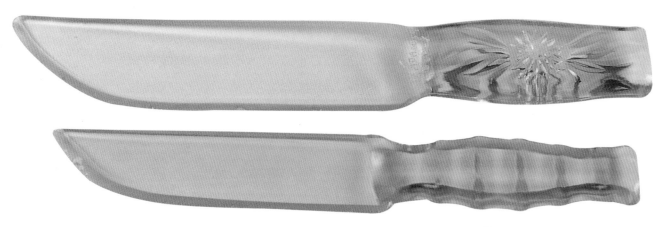

Knives. Dur-X. The top knife is 9.25" in length and marked "MADE IN U.S.A." on one side and "PAT. D. 112059" and "DUR-X" on the other. The 8.25" long knife is unmarked, but probably Dur-X. $60 each. *Courtesy of Walt Lemiski – Waltz Time Antiques.*

Refrigerator dish and butter dishes. Unknown manufacturers. Left to right: the 5.25" x 3.25" x 4" deep refrigerator dish came free with the purchase of a Norge refrigerator; the one-pound butter dish has a base 7.5" (handle to handle) x 4.5" and is 4" tall; the 6" x 4" x 4" deep one-pound butter dish has a subtle horizontally ribbed optic. Refrigerator dish, $45; butter dishes, $75 each. *Courtesy of Walt Lemiski – Waltz Time Antiques.*

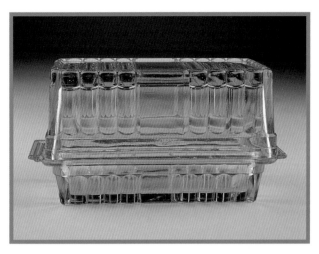

Butter dish. Unknown manufacturer. From Australia, a one-pound butter dish has the follow measurements: base, 6.75" x 3.5" x 1" deep; lid, 6" x 3.25" x just over 2". $250. *Courtesy of Sharon M. McGuire.*

Fish bowls. Unknown manufacturer. Left: 5" deep, 5" opening; right: 4.25" deep; 3.5" opening. $60 each. *Courtesy of Walt Lemiski – Waltz Time Antiques.*

Salt box. Sneath Glass Company. This was an open salt box that never had a lid. $250. *Courtesy of Clark Crawford.*

Towel bar. Unknown manufacturer. An 18" long towel bar with an unusual twist retains original brackets. $125. *Courtesy of Walt Lemiski – Waltz Time Antiques.*

Ice cube breaker. North Brothers Manufacturing Company. The 4.25" square, 3" deep glass reservoir was designed to store ice cubes in the refrigerator. This was sold as shown here for $3.75 in 1933 making it quite a luxury. $85. *Courtesy of Walt Lemiski – Waltz Time Antiques.*

Sundae glasses. Paden City Glass Manufacturing Company, U.S. Glass Company, and unknown manufacturers.
Left to right: Paden City 6" tall, 4.5" wide; U.S. Glass 6.5" tall, 3.25" wide; unknown manufacturer 6.5" tall, 3.5"
wide with a scalloped foot; Paden City 6.75" tall, almost 3.5" wide; Paden City 6.75" tall, 3.5" wide. $35 each.
*Courtesy of Walt Lemiski – Waltz Time Antiques.*

Tumbler, sundae glass, and drawer pull. Unknown manufacturers. The Thomas Jefferson commemorative tumbler is 4.5" tall and 3" in diameter. The 6" tall, 5" diameter sundae glass may be a Paden City Glass Company item. The 4" long drawer pull retains original hardware. Tumbler, $150; sundae glass, $35; drawer pull, $14. *Courtesy of Keith and Judy Hendrix.*

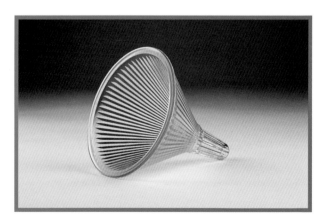

Funnel. Unknown manufacturer. Glass funnels are most commonly found in crystal (clear). This example is 4.25" in diameter and 5" long. $150. *Courtesy of Keith and Judy Hendrix.*

Mug. Unknown manufacturer. This 5.5" tall, 2.75" diameter mug is also referred to as a beer mug. $40. *Courtesy of Walt Lemiski – Waltz Time Antiques.*

Ladles. Unknown manufacturers. Left to right: 5" long, .75" rim; 5" long, almost 1" rim; 5" long, just over 1" rim with a slightly rounded bottom; 4.75" long with a round bowl and no real rim; 5.5" long, .75" rim with a flat area on the very bottom of the bowl; 5.25" long, .75" rim; 5" long, almost 1" rim with gold trim. $20 each. *Courtesy of Walt Lemiski – Waltz Time Antiques.*

Cruets. U.S. Glass Company and The Cambridge Glass Company. Left to right: 7" tall from the Cambridge 3400 Line, 6.5" tall by U.S. Glass, and 4.5" tall by Cambridge. Left to right: $95, $55, $50. *Courtesy of Walt Lemiski – Waltz Time Antiques.*

Pitchers and measuring cup. Hazel-Atlas Glass Company. Left to right: Marked "A&J" on the base, this 5.25" deep, 4.5" diameter measure was designed for a beater top. Pints, cups, and ounces are shown on one side. The middle pitcher is 5.5" deep and 4.5" in diameter with "A&J PATENT APPLIED FOR" on the base and is also designed for a beater top. The 5" deep pitcher on the right is 3.5" in diameter. $50. *Courtesy of Walt Lemiski – Waltz Time Antiques.*

Ice buckets. Liberty Glass Works. 5" deep at the lowest point, 8" diameter at widest point and 6" deep, 5" wide. $75, $65. *Courtesy of Julia & Jim Retzloff.*

Butter or whipped cream tub and ice tub. Unknown manufacturers. The butter tub, on the right, is 2.5" deep and 4.5" in diameter. The ice tub is 4" deep and 5.75" in diameter. Both pieces have decorative cuts that may have been added after the glassware left the factory. $65 each. *Courtesy of Carol Korn.*

Percolator tops. Hocking Glass Company. These 2.5" tall percolator tops are a standard size that fits metal coffee percolators from this period. The swirled design is quite rare. Paneled, $12; swirled, $20. *Courtesy of Julia & Jim Retzloff.*

Cookie jars. Dunbar Flint Glass Company and Bartlett-Collins. The Dunbar cookie jar has a 6 tall base with a diameter of 4.5". The Bartlett-Collins cookie jar is 7.5" tall with a 3" diameter. Dunbar (left), $85; Bartlett-Collins, $175. *Courtesy of Julia & Jim Retzloff.*

Batter Set. U.S. Glass Company. The 6" tall pitcher held the pancake or waffle batter, and the 4" tall pitcher contained the syrup. The fact that lids, which were easily damaged by normal household use, are intact add to the value of this set. There was an under plate on which both pitchers sat. $175 each, with the lids being at least half of the value, under plate (not shown), $85. *Courtesy of The Attic Annex, Joyce and Jim Coverston.*

Decanter. Paden City Glass Manufacturing Company. 10" tall. $200. *Courtesy of Sharon M. Mcguire.*

Water bottle. Hocking Glass Company. 8.5" tall. $30. *Courtesy of Walt Lemiski – Waltz Time Antiques.*

Canister and bottle. Sneath Glass Company and unknown manufacturer. The 7" tall Sneath coffee canister is 4.25" x 3.75" at its base. The Deco water bottle is marked with "279" on one side and "3" on the other. It is 8.5" tall and the maker is a mystery. Canister, $250, water bottle, $65. *Courtesy of Keith and Judy Hendrix.*

Refrigerator dishes. Hazel-Atlas Glass Company. "Round Refrigerator Bowls" were made to stack. Each section is 5.5" in diameter and 2.5" deep. $75 as shown with three sections and a lid. *Courtesy of Walt Lemiski – Waltz Time Antiques.*

Refrigerator dishes. Hocking Glass Company. Four containers were designed to stack and reduce the amount of space required in the refrigerator with two small (about 4" x 4"), one medium (about 4" x 8") and one large (about 8" x 8") container. Small, $25 each; medium, $35; large, $45. *Courtesy of Clark Crawford.*

Vase. McKee Glass Company. This 7.5"
"Triangle" vase is hard to find in transparent
green. $400. *Courtesy of Todd Baum and
Jesse Speicher.*

Pitcher. Hazel-Atlas Glass Company. Listed
in company catalogues as the 9870 80-
ounce Blown Water Pitcher with ice lip, a
ribbed pitcher measures 8.25" at the
handle. Originally produced in crystal and
pink, this is also found in green. $65.
*Courtesy of Carol Korn.*

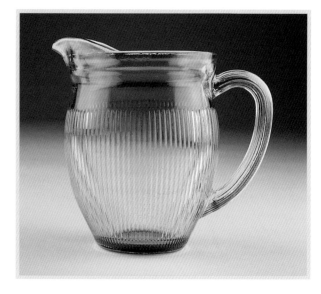

Pitcher. Hazel-Atlas Glass
Company. Known as the "Fine
Rib" pitcher, this was actually the
"9891 20-ounce Milk Pitcher"
that was originally produced in
crystal and pink. It is 4.5" tall at
the handle. $35. *Courtesy of
Lynn and Faye Strait.*

Pitcher. Federal Glass Company. This holds 85 oz. and was also made in amber and crystal (clear). $175. *Courtesy of David and Maryann Gaydos.*

Creamer. McKee Glass Company. This rarely seen pitcher is only 3" tall when measured to the top of the handle, and is part of the "Lenox" pattern of 1930. $35. *Courtesy of Walt Lemiski – Waltz Time Antiques.*

Pitcher and tumbler. Federal Glass Company. The "146 ½ R 65-ounce Jug" made in Rose Glow as shown and in several other colors is the "Lido Line." Tumblers come in four sizes: 5, 9, 10, and 12 ounces. Pitcher, $65; tumblers, $10 each.

Syrup pitcher. Hazel-Atlas Glass Company. A tin top covers this 6" tall pitcher that is marked: "HA 4K-803." This is one of many syrup pitchers made by Hazel-Atlas.

Cruets. Unknown manufacturers. These cruets are 6.75" tall and 8.25" tall. Small, $50; tall, $65. *Courtesy of Walt Lemiski – Waltz Time Antiques.*

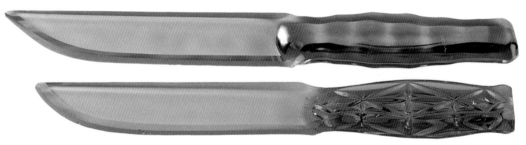

Knives. AER-FLO and unknown manufacturer. The 8.25" long knife on top is unmarked. The 7.25" long knife below is marked, "MADE IN U.S.A." and was produced by AER-FLO. $50 each. *Walt Lemiski - Waltz Time Antiques.*

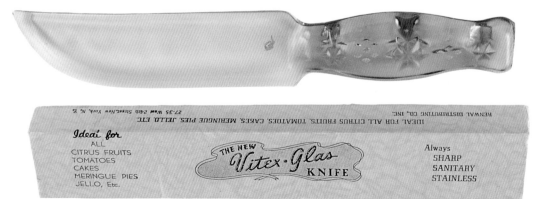

Knife. Vitex-Glas. 9.25" in length, this is unmarked. Add $20 for the original box in good to excellent condition and $10 more if the original tissue paper instructions have survived. $50. *Courtesy of Walt Lemiski – Waltz Time Antiques.*

Measuring cup. Federal Glass Company. Increments for third-cups, half-cups, and every four ounces are shown on this 3.75" deep, 5" diameter two-cup measure. $50. *Courtesy of Walt Lemiski – Waltz Time Antiques.*

Ladles. All are 5" long but other details are given left to right: .75" rim; .75" rim with a decorative cut in the bowl; 1" rim; 1" rim with a decorative cut in the bowl; almost 1" rim; round bowl with no rim; almost 1" rim. $25 each. *Courtesy of Walt Lemiski – Waltz Time Antiques.*

Batter bowl. U.S. Glass Company. The 8.25" diameter, 4.5" deep batter bowl is marked; "D & B Co." This has been nicknamed "Slick." $50. *Courtesy of Walt Lemiski – Waltz Time Antiques.*

Shakers. Hazel-Atlas Glass Company. These "1491" shakers were only made in Salt, Pepper, Flour, and Sugar. 4.5" shakers such as these are range sets for use while cooking. Care must be taken when selecting shakers for purchase as they have been reproduced. $85 each. *Courtesy of Dave and Hilda Proctor.*

Shakers. Damp Proof Salt Shaker Company, Inc. It is known that these 3" tall shakers were made by this Miami, Florida, manufacturer in an attempt to address the problems brought upon salt by humidity. Keep in mind that these were produced before the advent of air conditioning. Made also in green, one side is marked: "PAT 6 25 29" which refers to the patent date. The lids have the company name and patent date. $200.

Creamer and sugar. Hazel-Atlas Glass Company. These 4.5" tall cream pitchers and sugar bowls were free with the purchase of Kellogg's cereal. $25 each. Add $50 for original packaging. *Courtesy of Walt Lemiski – Waltz Time Antiques.*

Sugar and creamer. Hazel-Atlas Glass Company. The sugar was listed in Hazel-Atlas catalogues as "9856-9856 ½ Sugar & Cover." The creamer was number 9855. Both are part of the "Crisscross" line and were manufactured originally in crystal and green. As a later addition pink was manufactured for a shorter duration and therefore can be more difficult to find than crystal and green. Sugar base, $100; lid, $150; creamer, $100. *Courtesy of Dr. Dominic J. Menta.*

Refrigerator dish. Hazel-Atlas Glass Company. A 5" diameter, 3" deep bowl was utilized as a refrigerator dish with the addition of the hard-to-find cover. Listed as "9835-9835 ½" this is part of the "Crisscross" line and was introduced in crystal and green. As a later addition pink was manufactured for a shorter duration and therefore can be more difficult to find than crystal and green. $100.

Refrigerator dishes. Unknown manufacturer. The lid of these stacking refrigerator dishes is embossed with the product name "Kompakt," which refers to the efficient way leftovers can be stored using a minimal amount of space. $150 for the set as shown with two bases and one lid. *Courtesy of Dennis A. Busold, Robin's Nest Antiques.*

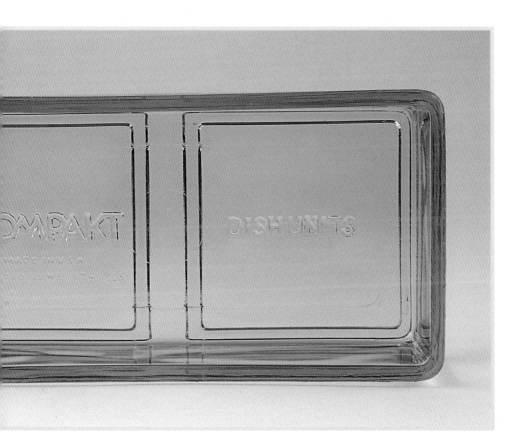

Refrigerator dish. Hocking Glass Company. This unusual piece is 4" x 4" x 2.75" deep. $70. *Courtesy of Dennis A. Busold, Robin's Nest Antiques.*

Sherbet. Thought to be Bagley. Measuring 4" in diameter and 3" tall at the peaks, this might have held a flower frog. The foot is exactly 2-³/₈" square. $12. *Courtesy of Sharon Nueske.*

Sugar dispenser. Sanitary Sugar Bowl Company. The base is 4.5" tall and 3.25" in diameter at the bottom, which features a molded star burst motif. The lid is marked: "SANITARY SUGAR BOWL COMPANY DESIGN PATENT 108945." $400. *Courtesy of Francee Boches, Cheshire Cat Antiques.*

Dessert dish. Tiffin – United States Glass Company. A box of Minute Tapioca or other General Foods products might have included the following: "A premium offer on Tiffin Minute Tapioca Dessert Dishes! Flush-Rose in tone-clear as fine-spun crystal-their delicate appearance belies a sturdy resistance to breaking. Tiffin is tempered for daily usage and long life!" The price? $1.00 for three, $1.35 for 4, $1.70 for 5, $2.00 for 6. These are one-piece items that are 6.25" in diameter at the base, 1.5" deep, and almost 4.75" at the rim. The green dessert dish is not mentioned in this 1930 offer. $18. *Courtesy of Edith Putanko (owner of) Edie's Glassware.*

Sherbet. Jeannette Glass Company. This item is particularly unusual as the foot features the Windsor Depression Glass design. One must assume this was a way to reuse Windsor molds. $12.

Cake plate. United States Glass Company. Named "Shaggy Daisy" by Hazel Marie Weatherman, this 10" diameter, three-footed cake plate was patented in 1930. $40.

# Red

Vase. Anchor Hocking Glass Company. Measuring 3.75" in height and 4" in diameter, this vase is often referred to as a "Squatty" vase. $18.

Batter pitcher. McKee Glass Company. 9" tall. $125. *Courtesy of Walt Lemiski – Waltz Time Antiques.*

Cocktail shaker. Unknown manufacture. Perhaps a Paden City item, this cocktail shaker is 10" tall. $85. *Courtesy of Walt Lemiski – Waltz Time Antiques.*

Shakers. Anchor Hocking and unknown manufacturer. The 4.5" tall shakers on the left are "Georgian" by Anchor Hocking. The 2.5" tall eight-sided shakers on the right feature glass lids. U.S. Glass Company made shakers with glass lids, but it is not known if these are by U.S. Glass as documentation has not been found showing the flat design seen here. Anchor Hocking, $60; other, $100.

Cocktail shaker. Anchor Hocking Glass Company. This cocktail shaker is one of two made in Hocking's Royal Ruby glass. This shaker is 9.5" tall to the top of the glass, and the other is 5.5" tall. $85. *Courtesy of Barbara Quick and Milton Quick.*

Beater jar. Unknown manufacturer. The glass has no indication of its source, but the beater top is an A&J product. $150.

119

# Ultramarine

Pitcher. Jeannette Glass Company. From the Jennyware line of kitchen glass, this pitcher measures 5" tall at the handle. $65. *Courtesy of Walt Lemiski – Waltz Time Antiques.*

Cheese dish. Unknown manufacturer. The 5" square base is shown in ultramarine but can be found in cobalt blue, red, and green. The lid is always clear measuring 2.5" tall to the top of the finial. $35. *Courtesy of Walt Lemiski – Waltz Time Antiques.*

Schiffer
Publishing
**Your Source for
Books on Glass**

# White —
# Milk Glass,
# Vitrock,
# and White

Bowl. McKee Glass Company. The Pennsylvania Dutch motif is shown on a 6" diameter, 3.25" deep "bell" bowl. A complete set of bowls is available with this design. $40 each

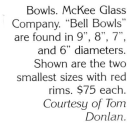

Bowls. McKee Glass Company. "Bell Bowls" are found in 9", 8", 7", and 6" diameters. Shown are the two smallest sizes with red rims. $75 each. *Courtesy of Tom Donlan.*

Bowls. McKee Glass Company. "Diamond Check" bowls are difficult to find in any color. These "Bell Bowls" are 9" and 7" in diameter. 9" bowl, $125, 7" bowl, $100. *Courtesy of Tom Donlan.*

Shakers. McKee Glass Company. "Diamond Check" Roman Arch shakers are difficult to find in any color. Missing are Flour and Sugar. $150 each. *Courtesy of Tom Donlan.*

Shakers. McKee Glass Company. "Diamond Check" Roman Arch shakers are difficult to find in any color. Missing is Salt. $130 each. *Courtesy of Tom Donlan.*

Butter dish. McKee Glass Company. "Diamond Check" one-pound butter dishes are difficult to find in any color. The base measures 5.5" x 3" and the lid measures 5" x 3" x 1.5" tall. $450. *Courtesy of Tom Donlan.*

Shakers and butter dish. McKee Glass Company. The Abraham Lincoln motif is quite elusive. Butter dish, $150; shakers, $125 each. *Courtesy of Tom Donlan.*

Butter dish. McKee Glass Company. Bowdle Live Stock Sales Company advertised on a clear-lidded butter dish. $125. *Courtesy of Tom Donlan.*

Refrigerator dishes, measuring cups, reamer, butter dish. Hazel-Atlas Glass Company. All of the items shown in this grouping were introduced in 1929 and now are quite rare. Back row: 3.5" tall one-cup measure with three spouts, "O-3038 Three Lipped Pint Measuring Pitcher," $125; 3.75" tall two-cup measure, "O-3042 Measuring Pitcher," $125; with a reamer top, "O-2954 Perforated Reamer," $75; front row: 6" diameter, 2.5" deep round "covered refrigerator jar," $125; 4.5" x 6" (handle to handle) x 2" deep, $125; 7" (handle to handle) x 3.75" x 3.25" tall one pound butter dish, "O-2013-13½ Butter Dish," $175. *Courtesy of Todd Baum and Jesse Speicher.*

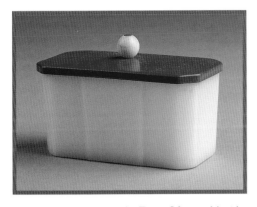

Grease jar or butter dish. Tipp. Often sold with shakers, this 4" x 2" x 2" container is hard to find and even harder to find with original decorations. Plain, $80; decorated, $250+. *Courtesy of Tom Donlan.*

Shakers, grease jar. Hazel-Atlas Glass Company. 4.5" tall shakers are paired with the rarely seen 4.5" x 2.5' x 2.5" deep grease jar. Shakers, $65 each; grease jar, $300. *Courtesy of Todd Baum and Jesse Speicher.*

Bowl and grease jars. Vitrock by Hocking Glass Company. The 8" diameter, 1.5" deep bowl is quite rare. 5.75" diameter, 2.75" tall grease jars are found in a variety of striped decorations and color combinations. The advertisement for "FAIRMONT'S BETTER "Patty Roll" BUTTER" enhances the value of an otherwise common grease jar. Bowl, $25; striped grease jar, $50; advertising grease jar, $150.

Bowls. Fire-King by Anchor Hocking Glass Company. These chili bowls are about 5" in diameter and feature red diamond variations. The design on the left, although not common, is easier to find than the design on the right. $20 each.

Bowl. McKee Glass Company. This is the smallest Red Ship bowl made measuring only 4" in diameter and 2.75" deep. For additional Red Ship items see *Mauzy's Kitchen Glass*. $40.

Bowls. PYREX®. Cinderella bowls with the Butterprint motif are most often found with turquoise designs, are sometimes found with pink designs, and are rarely found with yellow designs. From largest to smallest the bowls are: number 444, 4-quart, 10.5" x 4.5" deep; number 443, 2.5-quart, 8.75" x 4" deep; number 442, 1.5-quart, 7.5" x 3.5" deep, number 441, 1.5-pint, 5.75" x 3" deep. Cinderella bowls have tab handles that double as pouring spouts. $30 each in yellow, $25 each in pink, $15 each in turquoise.

Bowl. Hazel-Atlas Glass Company. The 5" diameter, 3" deep bowl is for children. The same mold was used as the base for Hazel-Atlas's Dutch Design Covered Utility Bowl. Children's kitchenware is particularly popular if found in excellent condition. $45. *Courtesy of Walt Lemiski – Waltz Time Antiques.*

Bowls. Hocking Glass Company. These Vitrock bowls are particularly rare with the additional red trim. The measurements from smallest to largest are: 6.75" diameter, 2.75" deep; 7.5" diameter, 3.25" deep; 8.75" diameter, 3.5" deep; 9.75" diameter, 4" deep; 10.5" diameter, 4.75" deep. $30 each. *Courtesy of Walt Lemiski – Waltz Time Antiques.*

Bowls. Vitrock by Hocking Glass Company. The largest bowl has a 9" diameter and 4.5" depth and the other two "nest" inside. $30 each. *Courtesy of Tom Donlan.*

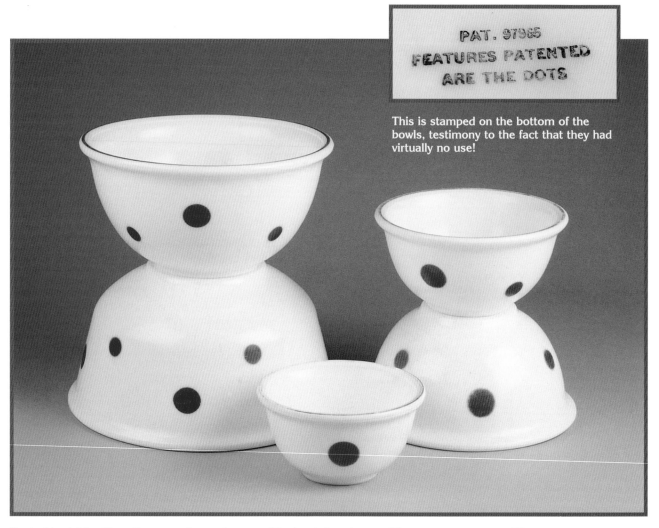

PAT. 97985
FEATURES PATENTED
ARE THE DOTS

This is stamped on the bottom of the
bowls, testimony to the fact that they had
virtually no use!

Bowls. Hazel-Atlas Glass Company. A complete set of five bowls is quite rare. The measurements are: 5"
diameter, 2.5" deep; 6" diameter, 3" deep; 7" diameter, 3.5" deep; 8" diameter, 4" deep; 9" diameter, 4.5" deep.
Careful observation will reveal a slightly different, straighter shape of the largest bowl, which is the same one
used by Hazel-Atlas for the Skaters, Dutch decorations, and more. $100 each. *Courtesy of Todd Baum and
Jesse Speicher.*

Bowls. Fire-King by Anchor Hocking Glass Company. Three
"Colonial Rim" bowls in one-, two-, and three-quart
capacities were sold together. $10 each. Add $20 for
original packaging.

Shaker and bowl. Hazel-Atlas Glass Company. The 4.25"
tall shaker is paired with a 9" diameter, 4.5" deep mixing
bowl in a two-color motif that is nearly impossible to find.
$250 each. *Courtesy of Todd Baum and Jesse Speicher.*

Bowl and sugar box. Hazel-Atlas Glass Company and Medco. The 8.75" diameter, 4.25" deep bowl is a Hazel-Atlas item. The markings on the sugar box are on the metal lid: "MADE IN U.S.A. MEDCO. N.Y." It is 4.5" in diameter and 3" deep. $45 each. *Courtesy of Walt Lemiski – Waltz Time Antiques.*

Bowls. Federal Glass Company. Federal made fewer bowls in white than Hazel-Atlas, McKee, or Hocking. The bowls shown here were decorated with a variety of motifs. $12 each.

Bowls and measuring cup.
Hazel-Atlas Glass Company.
The mixing bowls are 8"
diameter and 3.75" deep and
6" in diameter and 2.75"
deep. The matching 2-cup
measure is 3.75" tall. The
design on these Ovide pieces
is not in great demand at this
time. Bowls, $25 each;
measuring cup, $45. *Courtesy
of Gary Geiselman.*

Refrigerator dishes and bowls.
Hazel-Atlas Glass Company.
Round refrigerator bowls, as
they were originally called,
were designed to stack and
reduce the amount of space
required in the refrigerator.
Found in transparent colors,
the Ovide motif here is harder
to find but not in great demand
at this time. The refrigerator
bowls are 5.75" in diameter
and 2.5" deep. Shown with the
bowls is a 5" berry bowl that is
1.25" deep and a 5" cereal
bowl that is 2.25" deep.
Refrigerator dish (base only),
$15; lid, $15; berry bowl, $10;
cereal bowl, $15. *Courtesy of
Gary Geiselman.*

Refrigerator dish and batter
bowl. Fire-King by Anchor
Hocking Glass Company.
More common in jade-ite
these white pieces feature a
floral and leaf motif. The
refrigerator dish is found in a
smaller 4" x 4" size and always
has a clear lid. Refrigerator
dish, $75 in either size; batter
bowl, $125. *Courtesy of Tom
Donlan.*

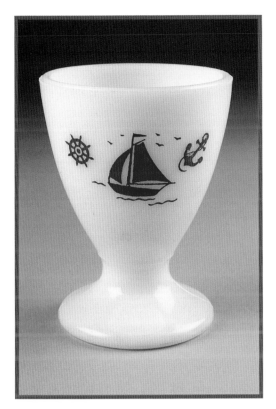

Tumbler. McKee Glass Company. 4.25" tall, 3.25" diameter, Red Ship pieces are much easier to find than black, but this is one of the more elusive red items. $75.

Refrigerator dishes: Hazel-Atlas Glass Company. Round refrigerator bowls, as they were originally called, were designed to stack and reduce the amount of space required in the refrigerator. These are decorated with fine bands of green. Another decorative treatment is on page 130. Refrigerator dish (base only), $15; lid, $15.
*Courtesy of Walt Lemiski – Waltz Time Antiques.*

Mug and tumbler. Hazel-Atlas Glass Company. Child's dinnerware is very collectible. Mugs as the just over 3" tall one shown here are not uncommon while the almost 4" tall tumbler decorated with "The Old Woman in the Shoe" is quite rare. The mug is part of the "Looney Tunes" Infant's Ware and has a matching deep dish (bowl) and divided plate. Mug, $20; tumbler, $45.

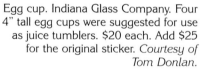

Egg cup. Indiana Glass Company. Four 4" tall egg cups were suggested for use as juice tumblers. $20 each. Add $25 for the original sticker. *Courtesy of Tom Donlan.*

Egg cup. Westmoreland Glass. 3.5" tall, 2.75" diameter. $20. Add $8 for the original sticker.

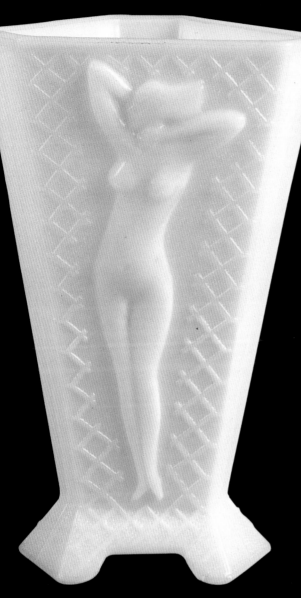

Vase. McKee Glass Company. The 7.5"
tall "Triangle" vase is quite difficult to
find in white. $700. *Courtesy of Todd
Baum and Jesse Speicher.*

Vase. McKee Glass Company. The "Modern Square" design is on this 8" tall, 6.5"
diameter vase. $250. *Courtesy of Todd
Baum and Jesse Speicher.*

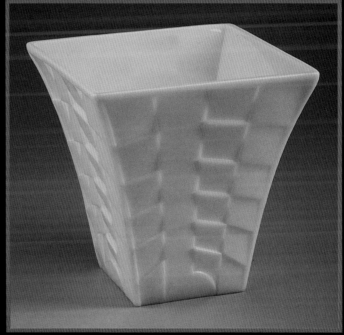

Napkin holder. Fort Howard Paper Co.
Measuring 4.5" x 2.25" x 3.5", the
manufacturing information of this napkin
holder is embossed on both sides. $250.
*Courtesy of Russ and Ann Dippon.*

Rolling Pin. Unknown manufacturer. There are no manufacturer's markings on this 18" long rolling pin that has wooden handles with worn, original paint. $180. *Courtesy of Walt Lemiski – Waltz Time Antiques.*

Coffee Carafe. McKee Glass Company. Glasbake was a McKee line of ovenware. A red Bakelite handle enhances the appeal of this coffee pot. $85. *Courtesy of Tom Donlan.*

DELUXE DUSTING POWDER by Coty NEW YORK PARIS Net Wt. 10 ozs.

Candy dish or powder box: Anchor Hocking Glass Company. Coty dusting powder was packaged in this glass jar that became a candy dish when empty. $85 unused with original tag.

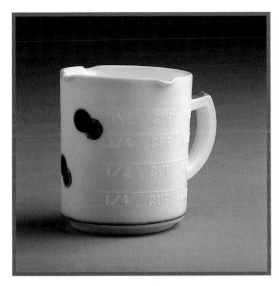

Measuring cup. Hazel-Atlas Glass Company. The 3.5" tall "O-3038 Three Lipped Pint Measuring Pitcher" was introduced in white glass in 1929. Variations add to the value of this item and polka dots in multiple colors are among the most elusive of motifs. $225. *Courtesy of Tom Donlan.*

Reamer and measuring cup. Vitrock by Hocking Glass Company. A reamer sits on a two-cup measure that has increments for half-cups and every four ounces on one side and third-cups on the other. The base of the measuring cup is marked "VITROCK." Reamer, This was the "O-3042-2954 Measuring Pitcher with Perforated Reamer" introduced in 1929 in plain white. The first catalogue number refers to the measuring cup and the second number to the reamer top. Reamer, $15; measuring cup, $45. *Courtesy of Walt Lemiski – Waltz Time Antiques.*

Shakers. Vitrock by Hocking Glass Company. 4.75" tall shakers were labeled with Salt, Pepper, Flour, and Sugar. The label on the far left is a new, replacement sticker. Although the lettering is similar, the letters are smaller and the background too shiny. Most collectors would rather have a worn original label than a gaudy new label. $10 each. Add $5 for an original label in good condition as shown. Add $15 for the original Vitrock sticker on the middle shaker. *Courtesy of Walt Lemiski – Waltz Time Antiques.*

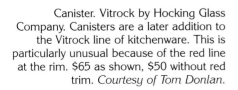

Canister. Vitrock by Hocking Glass Company. Canisters are a later addition to the Vitrock line of kitchenware. This is particularly unusual because of the red line at the rim. $65 as shown, $50 without red trim. *Courtesy of Tom Donlan.*

Shakers. Unknown manufacturers. Presumed to be Hocking, these shakers illustrate the variety of shapes from which homemakers could select. Paper labels indicate that these were purchased already filled with black pepper, nutmeg, and cloves; the shaker was "free." Left to right the heights are 5", 4", and 5.5". Add $10 to each shaker's value for original labels in excellent condition. $20 each. *Courtesy of Walt Lemiski – Waltz Time Antiques.*

Shakers. Tipp. 4.25" tall shakers have cherries on all four sides enhancing their value. $45 each. *Courtesy of Tom Donlan.*

136

Shakers. Tipp. Shakers are shown in two sizes, 2.75" tall and 4.25" tall, in original metal racks or carriers. The values of Tipp shakers vary tremendously based on the frequency they are found. Flower baskets are fairly common but butterflies are relatively rare. Flower baskets, $35 each; butterflies, $75 each. Add $15 for racks in excellent condition. *Courtesy of Walt Lemiski – Waltz Time Antiques.*

Shakers. Tipp. 4.5" tall with original rack. $75 each. Add $15 for the rack. *Courtesy of Todd Baum and Jesse Speicher.*

Shakers. Tipp. 2.75" tall shakers are shown in the original cardboard store display. The values of Tipp shakers vary tremendously based on the frequency they are found; the value here is really in the packaging as the Dutch shakers shown are among the most common Tipp shakers. Pepper, $15; Salt, $18; Sugar, $22. Add $40 for original packaging. *Courtesy of Francee Boches, Cheshire Cat Antiques.*

Shakers. Tipp. "Cock o' the walk" shakers are unmarked, so without the original packaging for these 3.5" tall shakers the manufacturer would remain a mystery. There are many shakers and additional accessories in this motif. $20. Add $15 for the box. *Courtesy of Cheryl and "Tab" Powell.*

Shakers. Tipp. 2.75" tall shakers are shown in the original two-tier metal lazy susan. The values of Tipp shakers vary tremendously based on the frequency they are found; the value here is really in the rack and the fact that the lids retain *original* pastel colors. Two lids are in each of these colors: pink, green, blue, and yellow. The spices are: All Spice, Cinnamon, Cloves, Ginger, Mustard, Nutmeg, Paprika, and Red Pepper. Spices, $35 each with original pastel lids. Add $35 for two-tier holder. *Courtesy of Francee Boches, Cheshire Cat Antiques.*

Shakers. Tipp. The bases of these 4" tall and 2.75" tall shakers are marked: "TIPP USA." These are extremely rare shakers that were found in a Goodwill store! $200 each. *Courtesy of Cheryl and "Tab" Powell.*

Shakers. McKee Glass Company. These 3.75" tall Roman Arch shakers are prototypes that were never produced. The original factory sticker remains on the bottom. These are too rare to price. *Courtesy of Todd Baum and Jesse Speicher.*

This is the factory sticker on the bottom of the prototype shakers indicating "Shaker No. 37" and "Decoration No. 3."

Shakers. McKee Glass Company. 3.5" Roman Arch shakers feature the uncommon use of "Su" for "Sugar." Salt, Pepper, Flour, $40 each; Sugar, $100. *Courtesy of Todd Baum and Jesse Speicher.*

Shakers. McKee Glass Company. Roman Arch with orange polka dots are hard to find, particularly on white glass. Shakers, $175 each. *Courtesy of Todd Baum and Jesse Speicher.*

Shakers. McKee Glass Company. The graphic on this 4" tall Roman Arch shaker is quite unusual and found on only two sides. The other sides of the shaker are white with no design. $75. *Courtesy of Walt Lemiski – Waltz Time Antiques.*

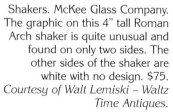

Shakers. Hazel-Atlas Glass Company. Glassware with polka dots is both popular and elusive. These shakers are 5" tall, or about 4" tall to the shoulder. Red dots, $150 each; blue dots, $165 each. *Courtesy of Todd Baum and Jesse Speicher.*

Shakers. Hazel-Atlas Glass Company. 4.5" tall "Shield" shakers were produced in a rainbow of colors but polka dots are quite rare. These were sold as the "O-155 ½ Square Kitchen Set." $175 each. *Courtesy of Todd Baum and Jesse Speicher.*

Shakers. Hazel-Atlas Glass Company. 4.5" tall "Shield" shakers were produced in a rainbow of colors but polka dots are quite rare. These were sold as the "O-155 ½ Square Kitchen Set." $175 each. *Courtesy of Tom Donlan.*

Shakers. Hazel-Atlas Glass Company. 4.5" tall shakers that are the same mold as the "Shield" shakers, but without the shield. This design with polka dots is quite rare. $125 each. Add $15 for the rack. *Courtesy of Tom Donlan.*

Shaker. Hazel-Atlas Glass Company. Here is a rare, perhaps one-of-a-kind, four-sided 4" tall shaker. There are four different black and red motifs with the word "sugar" on each of the four sides. This may have been a prototype never expected to leave the factory. Two pictures allow us to see all four sides of a piece that is too rare to price. *Courtesy of Todd Baum and Jesse Speicher.*

Shakers and light. Hazel-Atlas Glass Company. 4" shakers fit the rack on the base of a range light. Although the range itself was discarded years ago, someone had enough forethought to preserve this interesting arrangement. Shakers, $85 each; light, $50. *Courtesy of Todd Baum and Jesse Speicher.*

Shakers. Hazel-Atlas Glass Company. 4" tall in a rare design. $85 each. *Courtesy of Todd Baum and Jesse Speicher.*

Shakers. Hazel-Atlas Glass Company. 4" tall in a rare design. $150 each. *Courtesy of Todd Baum and Jesse Speicher.*

Shaker. Hazel-Atlas Glass Company. The rarely-seen flour shaker that accompanies the salt and pepper in the next grouping. $150. *Courtesy of Tom Donlan.*

Shakers. Hazel-Atlas Glass Company. Three pairs of 4" tall shakers feature unusual designs. $100 each. *Courtesy of Todd Baum and Jesse Speicher.*

Shaker. Hazel-Atlas Glass Company. Smaller than most "barrel shakers" this 3.5" tall shaker retains the original label and contents: Old Bay Brand Meat Seasoning." The shaker was "free" with the purchase of this Old Bay product. $12 for plain shaker, $50 as shown.

Shakers. Hazel-Atlas Glass Company. Smaller than most "barrel shakers" these six 3.5" tall shakers feature decorative graphics. $20 each. *Courtesy of Tom Donlan.*

Shakers. Hazel-Atlas Glass Company. The design on these 4.5" tall shakers is quite rare. $75 each. *Courtesy of Walt Lemiski – Waltz Time Antiques and Tom Donlan.*

Shakers. Hazel-Atlas Glass Company. 4.5" tall shakers can be found with the decorations in other colors. $50 each. *Courtesy of Tom Donlan.*

Shakers. Hazel-Atlas Glass Company. Glassware with polka dots is both popular and elusive. These shakers are 5" tall, or about 4" tall to the shoulder with a red dot over a black dot. $150 each. *Courtesy of Tom Donlan.*

Shakers. Hazel-Atlas Glass Company. These shakers are 5" tall, or about 4" tall to the shoulder and feature flower pots. $95 each. *Courtesy of Tom Donlan.*

Shakers. Hazel-Atlas Glass Company. These shakers are 5" tall, or about 4" tall to the shoulder and feature Flamenco dancers. $150 each. *Courtesy of Tom Donlan.*

Shakers. Unknown manufacturer. Miniature appliances are salt and pepper shakers. One can assume these were free with the purchase of the ice boxes they depict. $60 for the pair. *Courtesy of Walt Lemiski – Waltz Time Antiques.*

Shaker. Hazel-Atlas Glass Company. This shaker is 5" tall, or about 4" tall to the shoulder and found in Salt, Pepper, and Sugar. $95 each. *Courtesy of Tom Donlan.*

Shakers. Hazel-Atlas Glass Company. These shakers are 5" tall, or about 4" tall to the shoulder and feature a stylized flower pot. Missing is the Salt shaker. $95 each. *Courtesy of Tom Donlan.*

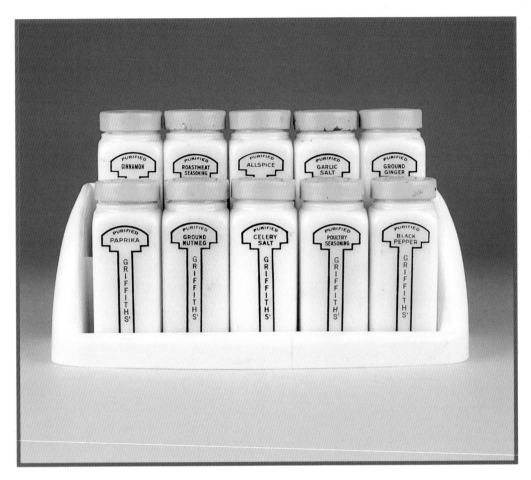

Shakers. Unknown manufacturer. Griffith's spices are easily displayed and retrieved in 3.5" tall shakers on a two-level rack. $8 each. Add $15 for the rack. *Courtesy of Walt Lemiski – Waltz Time Antiques.*

Shakers. Unknown manufacturer. Griffith's spices are easily displayed and retrieved in 3.5" tall shakers on a two-level rack. $8 each. Add $15 for the rack. *Courtesy of Walt Lemiski – Waltz Time Antiques.*

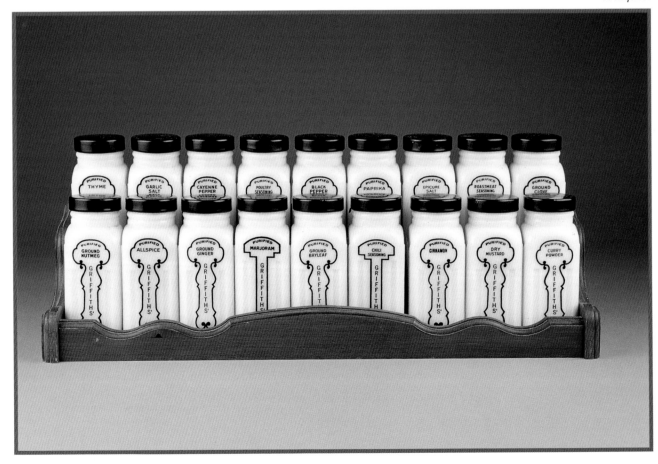

# White —
# Clambroth and Opalescent

Canisters and shakers. Unknown manufacturer. The larger canister was probably used for flour or sugar and the smaller canister was probably used for coffee or tea. The shakers would have held flour or sugar for use at the "Hoosier" cabinet while preparing to bake. Large canister, $85; smaller canister, $65; shakers, $55 each. *Courtesy of Clark Crawford.*

Shaker. Unknown manufacturer. Arches add texture to a 3.25" shaker. $50. *Courtesy of Walt Lemiski – Waltz Time Antiques.*

Canister. Unknown manufacturer. An original label remains on this 7" tall canister that has a 4.75" opening. $100. *Courtesy of Walt Lemiski – Waltz Time Antiques.*

Canisters and shakers. Unknown manufacturer. The design maximizes Deco styling in an appealing way.
Canisters, $300 each; shakers, $140 each. *Courtesy of Clark Crawford.*

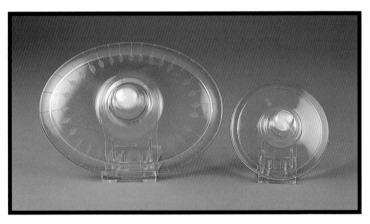

Lids. Fry Glass Company. Left: 8" x 5.75" marked "FRY 1932-8" for an
8" oval casserole; right: 4" round, unmarked for a bean pot. Left, $25;
right: $40. *Courtesy of Jack and Joyce Nichols.*

Cup and saucer. Fry Glass Company. Cup: 3.5"
diameter, 2.25" deep; saucer: 5.5" diameter.
These are unmarked. Cup: $30, saucer, $20.
*Courtesy of Jack and Joyce Nichols.*

Casseroles and trivet. Fry Glass Company. Left:
14" x 9.5" roaster. The base is marked: "FRY
OVENGLASS 1946-14 PAT. 5-18-17 PAT. 5-27-
19." Right: 8.5" round baker on a 7" trivet. The
base is marked: "FRY OVENGLASS 1920-8 ½
PAT. 5-8-17 PAT. 5-27-19. The trivet is marked:
"FRY'S HEAT RESISTING GLASS." Roaster,
$100; baker, $60; trivet, $85. *Courtesy of Jack
and Joyce Nichols.*

Tea Pot. Fry Glass Company. This is the rare individual tea pot with a 3" tall base having a 3" wide opening. The lid is 2.75" in diameter. $300. *Courtesy of Jack and Joyce Nichols.*

Patent dates are on the bottom of the loaf pan.

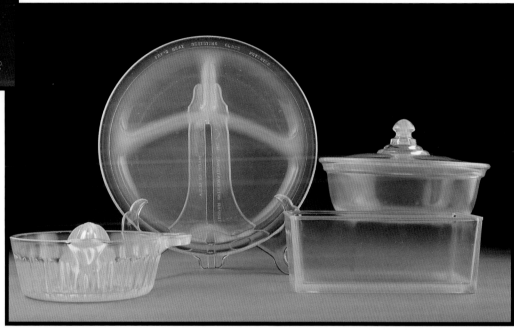

Casserole base, refrigerator dishes, and casserole in cradle. Fry Glass Company. Oval base: 9.25" x 6.75" x 3.75" deep and marked: "FRY OVENGLASS 1932-9 PAT. 5-8-17 PAT. 5-27-19." Stacked refrigerator dishes: 5" x 4" x 2" deep and 5" x 8" x 2" deep and marked "SPASO SAVO FRY OVENGLASS PAT. 5-18-17" with additional patent dates on the bases including: 2-11-18, 9-10-18, 5-27-19, 5-4-25, and 6-30-25. Note that the base of one dish acts as the lid for the piece upon which it rests. Casserole: 7" round, 2.5" deep base that is marked: "FRY OVENGLASS 1938-7 PAT. 5-8-17 PAT. 5-27-19." The metal cradle is unmarked. Oval base, $30; small refrigerator dish, $25; large refrigerator dish, $40; oval casserole with lid, $80; cradle, $15. *Courtesy of Jack and Joyce Nichols.*

Grill plate, reamer, casserole, and loaf pan. Fry Glass Company. Back row: 10.5" grill plate marked "FRY'S HEAT RESISTING GLASS PATENTED" and 8.25" diameter, 2.5" deep casserole. The base is marked "FRY OVENGLASS 1938-9 PAT. 5-8-17 PAT. 5-27-19. The lid is marked "1938-9." Front row: 6" diameter reamer that is 2.25" deep. 8.25" diameter, 2.5" deep casserole. The markings on the loaf pan is shown above. *Courtesy of Edith Putanko (owner of) Edie's Glassware.*

# Yellow — Seville

Vase, tumbler, mug, coaster, candy jar. McKee Glass Company. All with the nude theme, these pieces are from the early 1930s. The "Triangle" vases are 8" tall and 6" tall, and when a lid is added to the smaller vase it becomes a candy jar. . The 3.25" tall "bottoms up" cocktail tumbler is placed on the 4" diameter coaster. The "bottoms down" mug is 5.5" tall. Look for patent number 77725 on vintage tumblers and mugs. Vases $200 each, lid, $225; cup $175; coaster, $100; mug, $350. *Courtesy of Todd Baum and Jesse Speicher.*

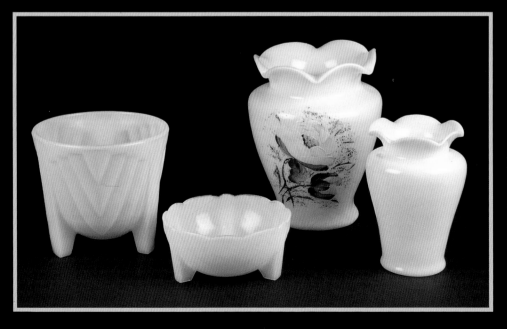

Jardinière, bulb bowl, and vases. McKee Glass Company. Left to right: 6" diameter, 5.5" deep three-footed No. 25 jardinière, 5.5" diameter, 2.5" deep bulb bowl, 8" Sarah vase, and 6" Sarah vase. Jardinière, $65; bulb bowl, $45; vases, $100 each. *Courtesy of Todd Baum and Jesse Speicher.*

Plate, shaker, and refrigerator dishes: McKee Glass Company. The three-part grill plate was styled after dinerware for use at lunch; "regular" dinner plates were utilized for the more formal evening meal. The Spice shaker is shown with others in this set in the following grouping. Square and rectangular refrigerator dishes more efficiently used ice box space than their round counterparts. Plate: $75; shaker, $85; small refrigerator dishes, $50 each; large refrigerator dish, $75. *Courtesy of Clark Crawford.*

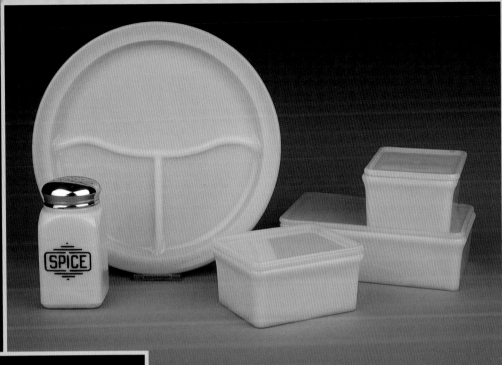

Refrigerator dish. McKee Glass Company. This box measures 8" handle to handle by 7.5" and is 3" deep with an unusual 7.75" square lid that has four tab handles. $125. *Courtesy of Todd Baum and Jesse Speicher.*

Shakers. McKee Glass Company. 4.5" tall square shakers with lettering sometimes referred to as "Deco lettering." Flour and Sugar, $70 each; others, $85 each. *Courtesy of Todd Baum / Jesse Speicher.*

Shakers. McKee Glass Company. 4.5" tall shakers in three different styles. The four shakers on the left have different lettering than the single Flour shaker. The matching foursome were sold as a set for $1.40. There are Salt, Pepper, and Sugar shakers that match the single Flour. The Pepper shaker on the right is distinctly unique and has a matching Salt shaker. Four matching shakers on left, $45 each; four shakers with lettering like the single Flour, $55 each; Salt and Pepper as shown on the far right, $85 each. *Courtesy of Todd Baum and Jesse Speicher.*

Canisters: McKee Glass Company. These 7.5" tall canisters have metal lids that snap or press on. $225 each. *Courtesy of Todd Baum and Jesse Speicher.*

There are no threads at the mouth of this canister because the lid is not screwed on but pressed into position.

Shakers. Hocking Glass Company. These 4.5" shakers feature script on an angle, a feature that always enhances the value. $75 each. *Courtesy of Todd Baum and Jesse Speicher.*

Canisters. McKee Glass Company. Rarely seen, the bases are Seville and the lids are black glass. Left to right: 6" diameter, 4.5" deep; 5" diameter, 3.5" deep; 4" diameter, 2.5" deep. $300 each. *Courtesy of Todd Baum and Jesse Speicher.*

Canister. McKee Glass Company. Red script greatly adds to the desirability of this 4.5" deep; 5" diameter canister. $150. *Courtesy of Tom Donlan.*

Bowls. McKee Glass Company. To maximize storage space these mixing bowls were designed to nest one inside the other. These were McKee's "3 Piece Mixing Bowl Set" that originally sold for $1.39 *for all three* in 1931. $75 each. *Courtesy of Clark Crawford.*

 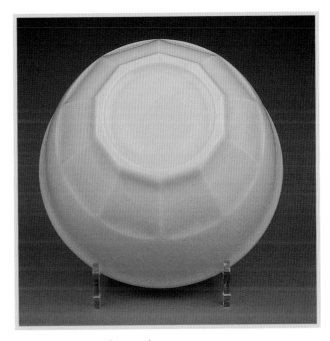

Bowls. McKee Glass Company. The details near the base of these bowls add to their value, as these are not often seen. A view from the underside shows how lovely this design is. $125 each. *Courtesy of Clark Crawford.*

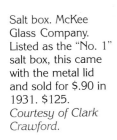

Salt box. McKee Glass Company. Listed as the "No. 1" salt box, this came with the metal lid and sold for $.90 in 1931. $125. *Courtesy of Clark Crawford.*

Drink dispenser and tumbler. Unknown manufacturer. Perhaps something a bit more decorative once occupied the space now shown with a cork. The clever design of this barrel-shaped dispenser includes metal holders for tumblers. The barrel is 7.25" long with a 4" diameter. The 2" tall tumbler is just over 1.5" in diameter. Dispenser, $200; tumbler, $15. *Courtesy of Kane's Antiques.*

# Bibliography

Florence, Gene. *Kitchen Glassware of the Depression Years*. Paducah, KY: Collector Books, 2001.

Grizel, Ruth Ann. *Welcome Home, Westmoreland*. Iowa City, IA: FSG Publishing Company, 1990.

Stout, Sandra McPhee, *Depression Glass Number One*. Des Moines, IA: Wallace-Homestead Book Co., 1970.

Stout, Sandra McPhee. *Depression Glass Number Two*. Des Moines, IA: Wallace-Homestead Book Co., 1971.

Weatherman, Hazel Marie. *Colored Glassware of the Depression Era 2*. Ozark, MO: Weatherman Glassbooks, 1970.

Weatherman, Hazel Marie. *The Decorated Tumbler*. Ozark, MO: Weatherman Glassbooks, 1978.

**Websites:**
http://zippy.cso.uiuc.edu
http://www.us-highways.com

# Index